Grasping Power

Grasping Power

Re-Thinking the Active Ingredient in Leadership, Education, Parenting, Global Survival, Forgiveness, Restraint, Identity

SCHUYLER TOTMAN

RESOURCE *Publications* • Eugene, Oregon

GRASPING POWER
Re-Thinking the Active Ingredient in Leadership, Education, Parenting, Global Survival, Forgiveness, Restraint, Identity

Copyright © 2021 Schuyler Totman. All rights reserved. Except for brief quotations in critical publications or reviews, no part of this book may be reproduced in any manner without prior written permission from the publisher. Write: Permissions, Wipf and Stock Publishers, 199 W. 8th Ave., Suite 3, Eugene, OR 97401.

Resource Publications
An Imprint of Wipf and Stock Publishers
199 W. 8th Ave., Suite 3
Eugene, OR 97401

www.wipfandstock.com

PAPERBACK ISBN: 978-1-5326-6350-5
HARDCOVER ISBN: 978-1-5326-6351-2
EBOOK ISBN: 978-1-5326-6352-9

04/12/21

To my father

[It is] a rather sad reflection on the present state of political science that our terminology does not distinguish among such key words as power, strength, force, authority, and, finally, violence—all of which refer to distinct, different phenomena and would hardly exist unless they did.

—Hannah Arendt, *On Violence*

Contents

Acknowledgments	xi
Preface	xiii
Here Is Little More Than a Glossary	
Five Cautions Before Proceeding	

SECTION 1: INGREDIENTS OF POWER

1   An Everyday Understanding of Power   3
Power Is Not a Polite Topic
The "Architecture" of Conflict
Regarding Other People's Power
Social Power Versus Individual Power
Individual Power as Social Power: Violence

2   Many Definitions of Power   15
Definitions of Power: Three Types
Leadership: Synonymous with Power
Dependence – Resistance = Actual Power

3   Many Forms of Power   23
Power Currencies: Hocker and Wilmot
Power Bases: Raven and French
The Carrot and the Stick: Trust-Based and Distrust-Based Power
*The Carrot **and** the Stick: Al Capone*
Converting the Carrot to a Stick
Setting-Based Power: Ecological, Normative, and Designated
Global Survival: Power Versus Influence

CONTENTS

4	**An Every-Person Appreciation of Power**	39
	Myriad Needs and Wants for Power	
	Differentiating Types for Goals	
	Identity Is Everything	
	Expectations: How Your Power Becomes Mine	
5	**An Every-Moment Awareness of Power**	47
	Sit Down: Power as Paraverbal, Nonverbal, and Proxemic	
	Text and Email: Moderating Relational Messages	
	Seriously but Not Literally: Power/No-Power Bids	
	Sharing and Unsharing Power	

SECTION 2: POWER IN CONTEXT

6	**Endorsement: Negotiating Power**	55
	Power Depends on Endorsement	
	Endorsement is Constantly Negotiated	
	Ongoing Endorsement	
	Endorsement is Instinctive	
	Endorsement: More Powerful than Power	
	Qui Tacet Consentire Videtur: *Passive Endorsement*	
	The Violent Caveat within Social Power	
7	**Regarding Other People's Power**	64
	Comparative Regard	
	Competitive Regard	
	Collaborative Regard	
	Designated Regard	
	Consumeristic Regard	
	Authoritarian Regard	
	Referent Regard	
	Insufficient Regard	
	Expansive Regard	
	Redlining: Self-Fulfilling Insufficient Regard	
	How Regards Define Relationships	
	Expansive and Insufficient Regards = Empowerment	
8	**Dependence: Power's Revealing Mirror**	75
	Involuntary Dependence	

Contents

Trust Building Before Involuntary Dependence
Violence and Involuntary Dependence
Voluntary Dependence: a.k.a. Trust
Soccer Parents on Dependence
Harvey Weinstein on Dependence
Dependence is Determined by the Dependent
The Principle of Least Interest: Waller and Hill
Salary as Dependence

9 Identity, Face, and Power   83
Facets of Identity
Face Concerns: Identity in the Moment
How Power Matters to Identity and Face
01/06/2021: When Facets of Identity Fight
John Wooden on Personal Identity
David Brooks on Personal Identity
Maya Angelou and Amelia on Personal Identity
Abraham Maslow on Personal Identity
Murray Bowen on Personal Identity
Don't Tread on Me: Negative Face Versus Power
Face Gain
Power Imbalance and Face
Identity and Manipulation
Identity and Resistance
Is She Coachable?: Resistance to Empowerment
"Culture Eats Strategy for Breakfast": Identity and Normative Power

10 Trust, Distrust, and Power   105
CBT, IBT, CBD, and IBD: Lewicki and Tomlinson
Trust-Based versus Distrust-Based Power
Trust and Distrust: High and Low
IBD, IBT, and Facets of Identity
High IBT: The Power of Collective Identity
Extreme IBD: Hate can be More Than Just Hate
When IBT is Violated: Betrayal
Forgiveness as an Act of Power
When IBD Is Violated: Best Picture

Contents

11 Given Authority Versus All Other Types   120
Given Authority and Coercive Power
The Eternal Yesterday: Five Sources of Given Authority
*Is Given Authority **My** Authority?*
Don't Expect Too Much from Given Authority
Two Ironies of Given Authority
Authority: Bridging Trust and Distrust

12 Self-Imposed Dangers of High Power   132
The Power Paradox: Keltner
Metamorphic Effects of Power: Kipnis
Two Kinds of High-Power People: McClelland
Future Abuse: Before I Kicked the Dog
The Dangers of Low Power
Schutz's FIRO–B: Your Power Meets My Needs
Consumerism: Society's Power on My Behalf
Destructive Symbiosis
With Great Power Must Come Great Restraint
The Irony of Henry V

Bibliography   145

Acknowledgments

The distance between a book with good intentions and a good book can only be traveled with the help of others. Several volunteer editors, proofers, and advisors covered that ground with me. Many thanks to Robin Capra, Stephen Petty, and William Nuessle for editing long sections, and then editing them again because I couldn't resist making extensive changes. When forgiveness suddenly became an important topic late in this process, Gary Hawk provided much prompt guidance and encouragement. Many thanks.

Many thanks as well to Clara Totman, Robin Capra, Robin Woolums, Lucy Mullen Davis, and Will Nuessle for your diligent review of final drafts. Clara Totman, Robin Capra, Kurt Menning, William Nuessle, and Thom Corrigan, thank you for the candid observations about the title and subtitles. I hope the adjustments (read: pruning) meet your approval.

Preface

Those writing books about power face two immediate challenges. First, they must address that power is not an attractive topic to write a book about. Power is an unpleasant subject for many. In the fifth paragraph of *The Power Paradox: How We Gain and Lose Influence*, for example, Dacher Keltner describes how we associate power most directly with "businessmen initiating hostile takeovers" and "bullies on the middle-school playground tormenting smaller kids."[1] Andy Crouch acknowledges in the second paragraph of *Playing God: Redeeming the Gift of Power* that "many people have a hard time thinking of power as good."[2] On the second page of *New Power: How Power Works in Our Hyperconnected World—And How to Make It Work for You*, authors Jeremy Heimans and Henry Timms introduce their concept of "new power" by contrasting it with a disturbing image of old power, Harvey Weinstein:

> Weinstein hoarded his power and spent it like currency to maintain his vaunted position: he could make or break a star, he had huge personal capacity to green-light a project or sink it. He shaped the fortunes of an entire industry—and in turn that industry protected him even as he carried out a decades-long spree of alleged sexual harassment and assault.[3]

These authors are wise to begin with this acknowledgement; books about power must recognize that the most obvious examples

---

1. Keltner, *Power Paradox*, 2–3.
2. Crouch, *Playing God*, 17.
3. Heimans and Timms, *New Power*, 2.

PREFACE

of it are vividly awful—chemical warfare, child sex trafficking, genocide. Anyone writing a book about power must quickly confront the understandable reluctance others may have to reading it.

The second immediate challenge faced by those writing books about power is deciding which definition to use. Power is a word with many different formal meanings.

Crouch adopts a definition from his colleague Ken Myer: "Power is the ability to make something of the world."[4] Keltner's is similar: "your capacity to make a difference in the world by influencing the states of other people."[5] Heimans and Timms, in the opening sentence of *New Power*, choose a more granular definition from social philosopher Bertrand Russell: "Power is the ability to produce intended effects."[6]

This book is more basic. It approaches the first challenge, but dodges the second. This book does examine power's bad reputation, and seeks to present a more balanced, constructive, necessary understanding. But instead of choosing one definition of power, this book presents several, compares them, and ponders the consequences of their coexistence. Power is one term that has accumulated many definitions. Consider a fourth, and how it contrasts the three already presented:

> *Power is the ability to change the behavior of others.*
>
> — Robert Vecchio

The four definitions presented so far illustrate key ways we recognize power very differently. Vecchio, for example, focuses on influencing other people. His definition is specific to *social power* only. Russell's definition accommodates both *social power* and *individual power*. My individual power is my "ability to produce intended effects" myself, alone, where my social power is my "ability to produce intended effects" by influencing others.

While Russell's definition might appear better because it encompasses both social and individual power, it enables a

---

4. Crouch, *Playing God*, 17.
5. Keltner, *Power Paradox*, 11.
6. Heimans and Timms, *New Power*, 1.

PREFACE

troublesome, even dangerous misunderstanding. Individual power should not be mistaken or substituted for social power. Where individuals *possess* individual power, "[social] power is the property of the relationship rather than the quality of the individual."[7] Social power is ultimately subject to negotiation by those being influenced, and must be.

Much of why we view power negatively comes down to this: one party resorts to individual power to force *intended effects* that should be negotiated, if at all, only through social power. Many of the worst terms we associate with power—slavery, shaken baby syndrome, terrorism, torture—describe one party employing violent forms of individual power to "change the behavior of others."

Similarly, we can use social power to "produce intended effects" only truly achievable through individual power, on our own. Self-actualization, for example, the highest of Maslow's hierarchy of needs, is achievable only internally, apart from others. Yet relational outcomes such as admiration, status, and belonging, all of which are achieved through social power, and all of which reside on Maslow's second tier, may well be more valued substitutes.

But, whether more valued or less, whether individual or social, in itself "power is neither positive nor negative—power just is."[8] In short, power is not the problem. Our differing, and often incomplete, understanding of power is more the problem.

Indeed, power[9] is a necessary, active ingredient in any social solution. Reconsider Vecchio's definition, "power is the ability to change the behavior of others." If valid, then power inhabits every act of teaching, coaching, encouraging, parenting, storytelling, leading, and mentoring future leaders.

And if Russell is correct—if power is "the ability to produce intended effects"—then power factors into every need, want, passion, cause, and ambition any of us has. And not just us. Every living thing that has wants and needs—dog, cat, horse, reptile, insect, plant—wants and needs power. (Yes, many of the concepts

7. Hocker and Wilmot, *Interpersonal Conflict*, 116.
8. Hocker and Wilmot, *Interpersonal Conflict, 9th ed.*, 73.
9. This book is concerned primarily with social power. Where it uses the term *power* without specifying, it is referring to social power.

xv

presented here help us appreciate how our pets negotiate with us.) "At an elemental level, all life exhibits power, transforming its surroundings. And all life requires power."[10]

And if the world-encompassing definitions from Keltner and Crouch are right, then your power and mine have global impact. Everything we make of this world, and everything we have made of it, for worse and better, depends on how we use our power.

And what if they're all right?

What if power is all of the above?

Then, at the very least, we'd benefit from a better understanding of it, and a careful awareness of how we understand power differently.

HERE IS LITTLE MORE THAN A GLOSSARY

This book's fundamental purpose is to improve our understanding of power by providing a glossary of power-related terms. Presented in these pages are roughly sixty studied concepts, along with definitions, descriptions, and practical examples to clarify and distinguish them. For example, this book presents many different kinds of power, noting significant differences between:

- social power and individual power.
- power and influence.
- given authority and earned authority.
- trust-based power and distrust-based power.

Further, Peter T. Coleman stresses that "it is critical to bear in mind that power is context-dependent and that even the most powerful people are powerless under certain conditions."[11] Therefore, this book also presents many context-defining factors, including different:

- forms and levels of dependence.
- forms of trust and distrust.

10. Crouch, *Playing God*, 17.
11. Coleman, "Power and Conflict," 1st ed, 124.

PREFACE

- facets of identity, and how each impacts one's need for power.
- ways one person regards another's power.

These context-defining and power-defining factors help us recognize the dynamics that make any specific circumstance unique and complex:

- What *ecological power* goes into building a prison, or setting up a classroom for special-needs children?
- How does the study of power shed light on profound, disparate dynamics like self-differentiation and forgiveness?
- How do the differences between social and individual power help us to distinguish forgiveness from reconciliation?
- How do *identification-based trust* (IBT), *identification-based distrust* (IBD), and *collective identity* coalesce to form powerful movements like Black Lives Matter and the Proud Boys?
- How might the strength of my personal identity mitigate my need for social power?

This book identifies and names dynamics most of us sense on an emotional, instinctive level more than we understand on a rational, conscious level.

And much power can come from this step of naming what we are sensing. Consider the following names:

- MeToo
- Deplorables
- LGBTQ
- MAGA

In each of these cases, a name united intensely felt individual perspectives. And in each of these cases, a strong collective identity coalesced. Naming can create community from isolation, shared identity from shame, unity from anxiety. The mutual, identity-fueled power that results can be immense. Global movements like those studied by Heimans and Timms hinge on naming.

Preface

FIVE CAUTIONS BEFORE PROCEEDING

The goal of this book is straightforward: present and define power-related terms, and clarify them with familiar examples. Many of these concepts will be grasped even before examples are provided. Others will require only a paragraph to establish a clear understanding. Ideally, the examples used will also be understood better through this process.

However, despite this simple goal, at least five interconnected cautions are merited before reading further. First, examining power, especially within context, greatly complicates power. Between the varying types of dependence, trust, distrust, identity, and power presented in these pages, a vast matrix of relationships forms. And each impacts all the others. How do my evolving personal identity and collective identity, for example, mitigate my need for specific forms of social power, which in turn impact how uneasily I both trust and distrust your authority?

Where do we start?

A second interconnected caution: it may be best to approach this book like a newspaper. Widely differing topics will be discussed on the same page. Many terms are introduced in early pages with only a brief description, and then combined in later chapters. Some readers may opt for a magazine approach; perusing the detailed table of contents or fanning through pages for specific subjects of interest.

A third caution: power impacts every aspect of our lives. The terms presented in this book illuminate complex, interwoven dynamics within ourselves and our relationships. Think of an X-ray image just as it is put up to the light. What was once a simple, gray rectangle suddenly teems with intricate detail. Interconnected parts instantly reveal themselves. The trained eye can then describe how parts work together, what is broken, and what is healthy. This book seeks to help train the eye.

A fourth caution: the terms presented here are not mutually exclusive. The same act of power—e.g., voting in an election—is an example of resource control power, referent power, individual power, social power, and the endorsement of power. Jim Crow laws exemplify ecological power, normative power, and designated power, and how these forms of power reinforce each other. A single fleeting act of power can be studied by many if not all the lenses provided in these pages.

The fifth caution: the terms presented here do mutually define each other. To better understand normative power, for example, it helps to understand collective identity, and vice versa. To better understand earned authority, it helps to understand the tension between identification-based trust and identification-based distrust.

Stating this final caution in practical terms, those concepts explored in later chapters modify and augment those introduced earlier. The reader must grasp these terms firmly enough to apply them, yet loosely enough to allow that understanding to expand as other concepts shed new light.

Distinct Ingredients, One Stew

It may help to liken this book to a stew recipe:

- These concepts are individually distinct, yet combine to form one fluid whole.
- All the concepts presented here can go in the same kettle, i.e. describe the same relationship at the same time.
- Those ingredients added later affect those added earlier.

And just as four different cooks will make four unique stews from the same ingredients, four different people will, by engaging these concepts differently, define themselves and their relationships uniquely.

Extending the stew analogy, this book is organized much like a recipe. It presents a list of ingredients first, and then describes how they come together. Specifically:

- Chapters 1–5 make up section 1, "Ingredients of Power." These chapters accomplish the basic goal this book seeks to achieve, providing lenses through which to recognize power dynamics in everyday settings. These chapters could be read in any order. (In fact, the author suggests starting with chapter 5.)

- Chapters 6–12 comprise section 2, "Power in Context." In these later chapters, connections and contrasts between power-related dynamics will be explored, and more complex dynamics pondered. For example, forgiveness will be explored as an act of individual power in which a person chooses how to adjust dependence, trust, distrust, and, perhaps most painfully, identity, in a process of mitigating the social power of another. These latter chapters are written assuming all the concepts presented in section 1 are understood well enough to apply, combine, and contrast.

You and I, for Example

When describing interpersonal relationships, scholars use a variety of pronouns to distinguish those involved: Person 1 / Person 2; Party A / Party B; LPG (low power group) / HPG (high power group). This book often uses *you and I*. For example, a sentence in chapter 1 states, "From a competitive, win-lose perspective, to gain power I must take it from you." These first-person pronouns are more efficient, and appear to the author to lend a realistic immediacy.

SECTION 1

Ingredients of Power

1
An Everyday Understanding of Power

The only way to predict the future is to have power to shape the future.
—Eric Hoffer

The power to question is the basis of all human progress.
—Indira Gandhi

Never forget that the most powerful force on earth is love.
—Nelson Rockefeller

When the power of love overcomes the love of power the world will know peace.
—Jimi Hendrix

Our sense of power is more vivid when we break a man's spirit than when we win his heart.
—Eric Hoffer

What it lies in our power to do, it lies in our power not to do.
—Aristotle

Section 1: Ingredients of Power

The sayings that begin this chapter form a patchwork discussion. The participants disagree, especially where Hoffer responds to Hendrix, but they don't contradict. Further, all do agree on the significance of power on internal, interpersonal, societal, and global levels. These sayings also illustrate how we understand power both differently and emphatically. If any of these statements is valid—and certainly if all of them are—then our future and our progress and our peace demand we carefully understand power.

POWER IS NOT A POLITE TOPIC

But before discussing power, it must be acknowledged that we generally don't like discussing power. Talking openly and directly about power is considered "bad taste,"[1] a sign of a distressed relationship.[2] Andy Crouch, author of *Playing God: Redeeming the Gift of Power*, recalls being repeatedly urged to use a less "abrupt and unsettling" term for his subject.[3] Further, this discomfort appears to increase as power increases. "People who hold high power positions are particularly prone to denying they have or use power."[4]

To be clear, we like power itself. "The overwhelming evidence seems to indicate that the powerful tend to like power, use it, justify having it, and attempt to keep it."[5] "Power is a dopamine high."[6]

We like power, we need it, and we constantly use power as we relate to each other. I just don't like talking about my power or your power with you. Instead we use many amenable but narrow synonyms—talent, skills, strengths, influence, etc. Power itself is often named only when referring to the harm it can cause. "Our culture's understanding of power has been deeply and enduringly shaped" by Machiavelli, who equated power with "force, fraud,

---

1. Kipnis, *Powerholders*, 2.
2. Ury, Brett, and Goldberg, *Getting Disputes Resolved*, 7–8.
3. Crouch, *Playing God*, 25.
4. Hocker and Wilmot, *Interpersonal Conflict*, 115.
5. Coleman, "Power and Conflict," 3rd ed., 153.
6. Keltner, *Power Paradox*, 7.

ruthlessness, and strategic violence."[7] Most people have heard Lord Acton's condemning caution: power tends to corrupt, and absolute power tends to corrupt absolutely. Yes, others do come to power's defense:

> *Power doesn't corrupt people, people corrupt power.*
> —William Gaddis[8]

> *There is nothing wrong with power if power is used correctly.*
> —Martin Luther King Jr.[9]

Yet even as these statements confront power's bad reputation, they are founded upon that reputation itself.

THE "ARCHITECTURE" OF CONFLICT

"In many discussions, the concept of power is linked only to the ability to overcome resistance."[10] This makes sense. Power has been called the "architecture"[11] and "structure"[12] of conflict. Careful study of conflict requires careful study of power.

Conflict, both in a static sense, e.g., the Cold War, and in a dynamic sense—then she did this, so I did this—can be dissected according to the sources of power each party controls. How we manage conflict has much to do with how we use—and refrain from using— power. As Aristotle said, what lies in our power to do lies in our power not to do.

Conflict can be employed to gain power or to establish power. A union may strike in order to gain increased revenue sharing. Two nations may engage in joint military training exercises, in part as a *show of force* to a hostile neighboring nation.

7. Keltner, *Power Paradox*, 2.

8 ⸱ Some quotations in this text do not receive citations. These the author believes to be commonly known as stated by the person they are attributed to.

9. King, Jr., "On Power and Love."
10. Deutsch, *Resolution of Conflict*, 87.
11. Folger et al., *Working Through Conflict*, 136.
12. Hocker and Wilmot, *Interpersonal Conflict*, 105.

SECTION 1: INGREDIENTS OF POWER

As these examples demonstrate, power may be the architecture of conflict, but it is very often the goal of conflict. An insecure person may *pick a fight* to convince others or himself that he has power. Indeed, any time someone loudly proclaims their own power, perhaps in the form intelligence or ability, it's reasonable to believe they don't thoroughly believe it themselves. As Margaret Thatcher said, "Being powerful is like being a lady. If you have to tell someone you are, you aren't."

Our National Pastime

Another reason we recognize power as it relates to conflict and competition is because, in general, we love power as it relates to conflict and competition. Football, baseball, horse racing, gladiators—throughout history, in any city or town, the venues with the most seats are those built to view and participate in competition.

And within these arenas, as contestants and spectators, we are most free to embrace that primal, Machiavellian urge to win by force, and even by fraud: *it ain't a foul if you don't get caught*. Where else can we so easily employ violent, bloody metaphorical phrases like *go for the jugular*, *dagger to the heart*, and *take his head off*? These familiar, popular settings thrive on the exhilaration of a competitive, win-lose regard for power.

REGARDING OTHER PEOPLE'S POWER

Competition is a part of everyday life, such as when kindergarteners race to get the best swing at the beginning of recess, or when employees are listed top to bottom on a board according to individual productivity. My "ability to produce intended effects" is very often determined by competing with yours. This includes the inner, identity-level delight I feel at getting a higher grade than you in Sociology 201.

But this *competitive regard* is just one of many contextual lenses through which one party can assess another party's power. Several common regards are introduced here and explored in more detail in chapter 7. Each brings its own assumptions and tensions related to how I believe your power impacts my power. How I regard your power is key to how I negotiate your power in our relationship.

Comparative Regard

Beyond a competitive regard, we constantly employ a *sociometric* or *comparative* regard, measuring whether we have high or low power relative to others. I constantly compare myself to others in society—am I middle class, upper class, upper-middle class, average height, college-educated? Are we *getting ahead, keeping up with the Jones, moving up in the world*? Within my organization, I may be middle management, entry-level, a Lieutenant Colonel, a subject matter expert. These examples illustrate how a comparative regard is, in many formal settings, necessary, beneficial, and clarifying. Resumes exist to help us compare one person's power to others.

On an interpersonal, identity level, a comparative regard may lead me to resist endorsing you. I may mumble congratulations on your promotion. Your pictures on Facebook of your family vacation to Tuscany may make me jealous. Terms like envy, jealousy, schadenfreude, and FOMO (fear of missing out) reflect a comparative regard.

Competitive Regard

Returning to the competitive regard, this lens is also comparative. But it goes further, viewing power as a scarce resource. Any power you have I don't have, and any power I want I must take from you. This orientation is called *zero sum* and *either-or*. Power is something to be won or lost. A competitive regard is necessary for sports, war, elections, sales department reward programs, and spelling bees. A competitive regard may manifest in fleeting situations, such as not allowing another person to change lanes in front of me.

Given how pervasive competition is in our lives, it may not be surprising that some people harbor a "chronic competitive approach to power."[13] Every situation gravitates toward winner and loser. This may manifest in an implicit need to *have the last word*, or to *measure swords*, or a tendency to see any disagreement as an attack. Internal needs—insecurities, low self-esteem, or a high need for validation—can drive me to constantly compete with others.

Collaborative Regard

Any act of teamwork requires a *cooperative* or *collaborative regard*. Your power increases mine, or at least doesn't reduce it. My colleague's expert power makes me more powerful. This is the regard we have for one another as we compete together against other teams. Nevertheless, scholars describe that while a collaborating regard is the natural orientation in some cultures, and "often the first choice of women in our culture," a competitive regard is more common to men and to U.S. culture in general."[14]

Designated Regard

Perhaps the most familiar lens through which we regard other people's power is a *designated regard*. "The President of the United States, police officers, managers at work, and professors all have certain designations of power in a particular role."[15] This is the regard we have for those to whom we have *given* authority. The unique dynamics of given authority will be explored further in chapter 11, along with five directions from which authority is given.

Authoritarian Regard

An *authoritarian regard* "involves an exaggerated need to submit to and identify with strong authority."[16] It may be more familiar to

---

13. Coleman, "Power and Conflict," 3rd ed., 152–53.
14. Hocker and Wilmot, *Interpersonal Conflict*, 9th ed., 124.
15. Hocker and Wilmot, *Interpersonal Conflict*, 10th ed., 119.
16. Coleman, "Power and Conflict," 3rd ed., 145.

An Everyday Understanding of Power

hear the term authoritarian referring to a person who holds power, e.g., an authoritarian dictator or an authoritarian regime. But an authoritarian regard describes the preference some have to respond to or even raise up a *benevolent dictator*.

> Individuals high in authoritarianism tend to favor absolute obedience to authority and resist personal freedom. These tendencies would most likely orient one toward either authoritarian or submissive orientation to power, depending on the relative status of the other party.[17]

Hence an authoritarian leader may expect submission from those he leads, but become submissive in the presence of another authoritarian leader.

Referent Regard

My *referent regard* comes from my admiration and strong identification with someone's charisma. I may reverence and identify with, or even idolize this person. I and want to behave, believe, and perceive in ways they approve. A ten-year-old girl displays a referent regard when choosing a role model, saying, "Someday I am going to be like her."

Consumeristic Regard

If I have a *consumeristic regard*, I want you to have power, and use it to meet my expectations. "Consumers give power away. They believe that their own needs can be best satisfied by the actions of others—whether those needs are elected officials, top management, social service providers, or the shopping mall. Consumers allow others to define their needs."[18]

The consumeristic, designated, authoritarian, and referent regards are all distinct forms of collaborative regard. These five regards share the orientation that your power benefits me. Hence all

---

17. Coleman, "Power and Conflict," 3rd ed., 145.
18. Block, *Community*, 63.

five can easily co-define the same relationship. This commonality will be explored further in chapter 8.

Insufficient Regard

An *insufficient regard* is illustrated by *helicopter parents* who believe their children will fail without constant supportive intervention. My insufficient orientation is my instinct to consider you incapable of achieving ends I value. Examples of an insufficient regard are common:

- The *mansplaining* boyfriend who gives his girlfriend pointers on knowing how to drive a stick shift, even though she's owned the car for years.
- The *micromanager* boss who keeps those reporting to her on a short leash.
- The *lawnmower parent* who goes ahead of his children and removes any obstacles before they can be challenged by them.
- The microaggression of assuming that since you look Asian I should speak English slowly so that you will understand.

My insufficient regard believes you don't have what it takes. Chapter 7 will discuss how this regard can be employed deliberately, even as a tool for sexism or rankism.

Expansive Regard

An *expansive regard* is demonstrated in a college classroom, an executive mentoring program, and when a mom practices with her daughter how to cross the street safely. Expansive settings exist to increase the power of others. Success is defined by how effectively I share my power with you. A student-teacher relationship increases the student's "ability to produce intended effects."

The expansive regard stands in polar contrast to the competitive regard. The competitive person increases power by taking it away. The person with the expansive regard increases power by giving it away. Where a competitive regard prompts the question "Who among us is the greatest?" an expansive mentor may say with satisfaction to her students, "You will do greater things than I."

SOCIAL POWER VERSUS INDIVIDUAL POWER

As touched on in the preface, we dangerously misunderstand power by equating individual power with social power. "Many theorists who have been concerned with power have focused on it solely as an attribute of the actor. This neglects its relational aspects and implicitly assumes that it remains constant across situations, an assumption that is clearly false."[19]

Individual power is that person's "ability to produce intended effects" alone, independent of others. Heather's extensive experience as a pilot and Scott's talent on the cello are forms of individual power. To be clear, individual power can be drawn upon as a social power resource. Heather's skills and experience may influence an airline to hire her. Scott may audition for an orchestra.

Social power involves the ability to influence others, making it subject to negotiation, and thus far more complex than individual power. My social power does not exist without your *endorsement*. Hannah Arendt was referring to social power when she stated, "Power is never the property of an individual; it belongs to a group and remains in existence only so long as the group keeps together."[20] Chapter 6 explores the constant, power-defining and sometimes power-denying process of endorsement in necessary detail.

Unlike individual power, social power can increase, decrease, and even disappear as other relational factors change, such as dependence, trust, distrust, interest, affection, and ability to resist. But two factors contribute to the mistaken assumption that social power is the same as individual power:

- A competitive regard for other people's power. Any competitive setting, especially those involving violence, is about

---

19. Deutsch, *Resolution of Conflict*, 85.
20. Arendt, *On Violence*, 44.

SECTION 1: INGREDIENTS OF POWER

overcoming others' power without their agreement. In competition, your power is established when you overcome my efforts to resist you. Especially when one party is *physically* competing against another—from a soccer match to military combat—individual and social power are effectively the same.

- *Outcome-based* definitions of power (described in the next chapter) encompass both individual and social power. For example, Bertrand Russell's definition—"Power is the ability to produce intended effects"—could be describing either social or individual power.

INDIVIDUAL POWER AS SOCIAL POWER: VIOLENCE

Nevertheless, confusing individual power and social power can lead to attempts to "change the behavior of others" simply by overpowering them. Might equals right. The most vivid examples of this involve violence. Any act of violence is an effort to make individual power synonymous with social power. Terms like terrorism, enslavement, physical abuse, robbery, torture, and rape name efforts to influence the state of other people by force, against their will.

Power Just Is

Yes, power is rightly associated with polarizing dynamics like coercion, competition, corruption, and conflict. And yes, sexual assault is really about power.[21] And yes, your fear of me can give me real power. All these realities help explain why power can be an unsettling subject.

But despite any notoriety, earned or unearned, "Power is neither positive nor negative—power just is."[22] A newborn's first cry is a reflexive effort to "produce intended effects." Again, "there is

---

21. Yonack, "Sexual Assault Is about Power," para. 1.
22. Hocker and Wilmot, *Interpersonal Conflict*, 73.

An Everyday Understanding of Power

nothing wrong with power if power is used correctly."[23] Referring to power as good or bad "is akin to classifying our breathing function as good or bad."[24]

Confronting the perception that power is equated merely with fear and coercion, Deutsch and Keltner respond similarly:

> *This seems too narrow a view. It overlooks the possibility that power can be facilitative as well as coercive, that it can liberate as well as restrain, that it can be "for" as well as "against."*
> —Morton Deutsch[25]

> *Perhaps most critically, thinking of power as coercive force and fraud blinds us to its pervasiveness in our daily lives and the fact that it shapes every interaction, from parents and children to those between work colleagues.*
> —Dacher Keltner[26]

Power is at work when good, great or small, comes from people seeking to "bring about intended effects," or to "change the behavior of others." Consider the Parable of the Good Samaritan: every benevolent, self-sacrificing act ascribed to the main character is an act of power. It is an act of power when:

- an eight-year-old girl specifies in her birthday party invitation that guests should bring items for the local animal shelter instead of gifts;
- a state trooper stops a driver for not speeding, and offers all the car's occupants ice cream as a reward;
- a drive-through coffee shop customer pays for the order of the driver behind him;
- a father counts to three and lets go of the bicycle, jogging behind as his five-year-old daughter pedals on alone, under her own power.

23. King Jr., "On Power and Love."
24. Hocker and Wilmot, *Interpersonal Conflict*, 73.
25. Deutsch, *Resolution of Conflict*, 87.
26. Keltner, *Power Paradox*, 3.

Section 1: Ingredients of Power

Power is all of the above. And the better we understand power, the better we understand our relationships, our impact, our opportunities, and our responsibilities within this world. "We can understand ourselves only through the lens of power."[27]

---

27. Keltner, *Power Paradox*, 14.

2

Many Definitions of Power

As is illustrated by the vast literature on power from philosophy, history, sociology, political science, and psychology, there are about as many conceptualizations of power as there are authors who have written on it.

—Peter T. Coleman

Like love, we know that power exists, but we cannot agree on a description of it.

—David Kipnis

People recognize power in widely differing ways. We may equate power with control, influence, authority, fear, ability, capacity, expertise, might, responsibility, manipulation, energy, servanthood, credibility, sway, dominance, autonomy, strength, charisma, skill, force, persuasion, impact, and/or leverage. These synonyms vary greatly, but power can be any and all of the above.

DEFINITIONS OF POWER: THREE TYPES

Definitions of power appear to fall into three categories: those that emphasize *outcome*, those that emphasize *relationship*, and those that emphasize the *connection* between these two, melding desired relationships with desired outcomes. How I perceive power, seek to use it, assume others use it, and expect others to respond to my power, all depend on which kind of definition I subscribe to.

Outcome Emphasis Definitions of Power

> *[Power is] the ability to influence or control events.*
> —Folger, Poole, and Stutman[1]

> *[Power is] the ability to make things happen or to bring about desired outcomes.*
> —Peter T. Coleman[2]

> *[Power is] the ability to achieve a purpose.*
> —Martin Luther King Jr.[3]

Relational Emphasis Definitions of Power

> *Power is deliberate or purposive influence.*
> —Morton Deutsch[4]

> *Power is the ability to change the behavior of others.*
> —Robert Vecchio[5]

> *Interpersonal power is the ability to influence a relational partner in any context because you control, or at least the partner perceives that you control, resources that the partner needs, values, desires, or fears. Interpersonal power includes the ability to resist the influence attempts of a partner.*
> —Hocker and Wilmot[6]

1. Folger et al., *Working Through Conflict*, 170.
2. Coleman, "Power and Conflict," 2nd ed., 121.
3. King, Jr., "On Power and Love"
4. Deutsch, *Resolution of Conflict*, 87.
5. Vecchio, *Leadership*, 69.
6. Hocker and Wilmot, *Interpersonal Conflict*, 117.

Many Definitions of Power

By social power we mean an individual's potentiality for influencing one or more other persons toward acting or changing in a given direction.
—George Levinger[7]

A person is powerful when he or she has the resources to act and to influence others and the skills to do this effectively.
—Morton Deutsch[8]

Connection (Outcome and Relationship) Emphasis Definitions of Power

Power is said to be exercised when changes occur in the target person's behavior that can be attributed to the powerholder's influence and that serve the powerholder's interests and intentions. Furthermore, these changes would ordinarily not have been carried out by the target person.
—David Kipnis[9]

Power is your capacity to make a difference in the world, by influencing the states of other people.
—Dacher Keltner[10]

Individuals have power when they have access to resources that can be used to persuade or convince others, to change their course of action, or to prevent others from moving toward their goals in conflict situations.
—Folger, Poole, and Stutman[11]

---

7. Levinger, "Development of Perceptions and Behavior," 83.
8. Deutsch, *Resolution of Conflict*, 87.
9. Kipnis, *Powerholders*, 2.
10. Keltner, *Power Paradox*, 11.
11. Folger et al., *Working Through Conflict*, 140.

SECTION 1: INGREDIENTS OF POWER

What Differences Do These Make?

Like the many synonyms for power, these definitions vary greatly. But they don't go quite so far as to contradict. Power can be any and all of the above. And each adds something to our understanding and appreciation of the others.

Further, whatever definition(s) of power I truly identify with determine(s) how I move through life. "Power is the medium through which we relate to one another."[12]

Still, these varied perspectives lead to practical questions:

- How might a person who sees power as the "ability to bring about desired outcomes" engage others differently than the one who recognizes that ongoing power requires the skills to use it effectively?

- How might a person who sees power as *control* view their surroundings differently than the person who sees power as the ability to make a difference in the world?

- How might a person who recognizes power merely as *fear* tend to regard other people with power?

LEADERSHIP: SYNONYMOUS WITH POWER

Three definitions of power are listed below, each representing one of the three emphasis types described earlier in this chapter. Adjacent to each definition of power is a respected definition of leadership. Note the near-synonymous meaning within each pair.

Relational Emphasis

Power is deliberate or purposive influence.
—Morton Deutsch

Leadership is intentional influence.
—Michael McKinney[13]

12. Keltner, *Power Paradox*, 2.
13. McKinney, "Leadership Quotes."

Many Definitions of Power

Outcome Emphasis

> *Leadership is the capacity to translate vision into reality.*
> —Warren Bennis[14]
>
> *[Power is] the ability to bring about desired outcomes.*
> —Peter T. Coleman[15]

Connection Emphasis

> *By social power we mean an individual's potentiality for influencing one or more other persons toward acting or changing in a given direction.*
> —George Levinger[16]
>
> *Leadership is the art of getting someone else to do something you want done because he wants to do it.*
> —Dwight D. Eisenhower[17]

While the outright synonymy seen in the first pair of definitions fades in the latter pairings, the similarity of meaning remains constant. For every respected definition of leadership, one can find a respected definition of power that makes the same statement. Hence, every act of leadership is an act of power, and the better we understand power, the better we understand leadership. This begs other questions, such as:

- How would a leader who equates leadership with "achieving desired outcomes" lead differently from the one who sees leadership as "the art of getting someone else to do something you want done because he wants to do it"?

- How would a leader who sees power as "the ability to produce intended effects" lead differently than one recognizes that

---

14. McKinney, "Leadership Quotes."
15. Coleman, "Power and Conflict," 1st ed., 112.
16. Levinger, "Development of Perceptions and Behavior," 83.
17. McKinney, "Leadership Quotes."

power involves both the ability to "influence others and the skills to do this effectively"?

Individual Power and Outcome-Emphasis Definitions

Social power is often equated with individual power. Outcome-emphasis definitions of power enable this, because they accommodate both individual and social power. One can "bring about desired outcomes," depending on what they are, via either social or individual power. Someone with an outcome-based understanding may reasonably consider both the same.

DEPENDENCE − RESISTANCE = ACTUAL POWER

Hocker and Wilmot's 2014 definition of power merits further scrutiny, because it draws attention to two significant, context-defining factors, *resistance* and *dependence*:

> Interpersonal power is the ability to influence a relational partner in any context because you control, or at least the partner perceives that you control, resources that the partner needs, values, desires, or fears. Interpersonal power includes the ability to resist the influence attempts of a partner.[18]

Resistance

Resistance is the power to oppose power, the *influence attempts of a partner*. It manifests in many forms, from physical and individual to hidden and systemic. Resistance can look like a trade union strike or a loud mob of protesters occupying a city's airport. But resistance is also Rosa Parks: simple, solitary, silent, unmoving.

---

18. Hocker and Wilmot, *Interpersonal Conflict*, 117.

Many Definitions of Power

Another keen example of resistance is seen in the systems theory concept of *balancing processes*, which describes a group's resistance to change:

> *Whenever there is "resistance to change," you can count on their being one or more "hidden" balancing processes. Resistance to change is neither capricious nor mysterious. It almost always arises from threats to traditional norms and ways of doing things. Often these norms are woven into the fabric of established power relationships.*[19]

The concept of balancing processes sheds light on how existing power structures resist those who seek change.

Leaders are often forged by leading resistance to established power. In fact, many iconic leaders in history—especially U.S. history—were forged in settings in which they resisted other established leaders: George Washington, Mahatma Gandhi, Cesar Chavez, Harriet Tubman, Jesus Christ, Winston Churchill, Martin Luther King Jr., Nelson Mandela, William Wallace, Abraham Lincoln. The enduring respect bestowed on these leaders attests to how we can venerate resistance to leadership as much as we do leadership itself.

Dependence

Hocker and Wilmot's 2014 definition of power focuses on control of "resources that the partner needs, values, desires, or fears." In short, your power is determined by my dependence on you.

Power requires dependence. You can end my power by somehow becoming *in*dependent, perhaps by increasing your individual power in some way. For example, one nation may work to end its dependence on foreign oil by expanding its domestic production or expanding its renewable energy options. A talented engineer may keep her resume current and accessible online, partly to make it easier, if necessary, to end dependence on her overbearing supervisor.

To understand the true power dynamics in any relational setting, one must study how each party depends on the others in that

---

19. Senge, *Fifth Discipline*, 88.

Section 1: Ingredients of Power

setting. The high-power party within a group may well be the high-dependence party as well. Dependence will be explored in more depth in chapter 8.

3
Many Forms of Power

Knowledge is power.
> —Francis Bacon

Character is power.
> —Booker T. Washington

Knowledge will give you power, but character respect.
> —Bruce Lee

Real power is, I don't even want to use the word, fear.
> —Donald Trump

Nearly all men can stand adversity, but if you want to test a man's character, give him power.
> —Abraham Lincoln

Just as there are many definitions of power, and many synonyms for power, there are many types of power. Phrases like *money is power, sexual power, military power,* and the *power of love* illustrate some of the myriad forms power can take. A "broad range of resources"[1] can be used to influence others.

---

1. Folger et al., *Working Through Conflict*, 140.

Section 1: Ingredients of Power

Scholars have worked to categorize social power into different types. Hocker and Wilmot's *Power Currencies* and French and Raven's *Bases of Social Power* are two such efforts. These studied categorizations are informative in themselves, and in how they contrast each other.

POWER CURRENCIES: HOCKER AND WILMOT

Hocker and Wilmot categorize power resources from a fluid perspective, as types of currency[2]:

Resource control: What do you have that I want or value, e.g., mineral rights to this land, your vote in the next election, money to donate to my cause? What *informal* resources do you control, such as approval or respect?

What can you provide or withhold that I need? Also, what can you make happen that I want to avoid? Can you fire me, arrest me, embarrass me? Resource control power encompasses rewards, but also coercion and formal punishment.

Interpersonal linkages: Whom do you know? Who are your friends? What is your network? "Your position in a larger system, such as being central to the communication exchange."[3] Interpersonal linkages help one attain power through coalition building, such as joining a factory worker's union. The family systems concept of *triangulation*, in which two parties stabilize and strengthen their relationship through mutual assessment of a third, illustrates this form of power.

Communication skills: Your skill on a verbal, nonverbal, and paraverbal levels, including your ability to speak with authority. "If you can lead a group in a decision-making process, speak persuasively, write a news release for your organization, or serve as an informal mediator between angry people, you will gain power because of your communication skills."[4]

---

2. Hocker and Wilmot, *Interpersonal Conflict*, 9th ed., 119–20.
3. Hocker and Wilmot, *Interpersonal Conflict*, 9th ed., 120.
4. Hocker and Wilmot, *Interpersonal Conflict*, 9th ed., 121.

Examples of coercive communication skills power include my ability to make you feel guilty or *shut you up with a look*. Communication skills power also encompasses the power to misinform or selectively inform. Editing an audio file to take a quote out of context is an instance of communication skills power, as is manipulating that audio file to sound like a different person. A good liar is demonstrating communication skills power.

Expertise: Some special skill or knowledge. This may be your experience and expertise on patent law, my ability to protect the quarterback's blind side during passing plays, or the *local knowledge* a sailor has of a certain section of coastline. I can use my expert power coercively by threatening to withhold it from those who need it.

POWER BASES: RAVEN AND FRENCH

Originally presented in 1959, and augmented up through 2012, Raven and French's "Bases of Social Power"[5] are a foundational and oft-used means to differentiate power.

Reward power: My ability to reward you.[6] What I can give you if you produce an outcome I desire or behave as I want. These may be *impersonal rewards*, e.g., an automatic bonus for reaching sales goals. I may also provide you with *personal rewards*, e.g., approval, interest, validation. Questions related to reward power include:

- Do I value the reward?
- Can I obtain it elsewhere?
- Does this actually reward my behavior, or does everybody get one? Is this just a participation trophy?

---

5. Power bases are commonly attributed with the name sequence Raven and French, possibly because Raven continued to augment them after original publication. But the definitions cited here rely on the original 1959 publication, listed as French and Raven.
6. French and Raven, "Bases of Social Power," 152.

Section 1: Ingredients of Power

Coercive power: The ability to punish, or threaten punishment.[7] A manager's authority to fire an employee and a state trooper's authority to write me a speeding ticket are examples of formal or *impersonal* coercive power. My ability to shame or demean you are examples of *personal* coercive power. Questions related to coercive power include:

- Are the consequences that bad?
- What are the odds of me getting caught?
- Is the possible punishment worth the risk?
- What subtle rewards might there be? A member of a street gang may receive elevated status for going to jail.

Referent power: Power derived from my identification with you. If I respond to your referent power, it comes from my "feeling of oneness"[8] with you. The more strongly I identify with you, the greater your referent power.[9] I admire you, am "highly attracted"[10] to you, venerate you, and consider you ideal in ways I value. Due to your referent power, I want to behave, believe, and perceive in ways you approve.

Expert power: The extent of knowledge, or perception of that knowledge, within a given area.[11] What valued insight do I have? Just like Hocker and Wilmot's *expertise power*, this power base can take many forms, from a professor's authoritative knowledge of climate science to a stranger providing directions to a coffee shop. *Perceived* expertise is all that is needed for expert power. A con artist can pass herself off as a doctor for as long as she maintains a trusted perception.

Informational power: Power derived from the effective use of information, including logic, rational argument, and persuasion. Raven and French distinguish informational power from expert

---

7. French and Raven, "Bases of Social Power," 152.
8. French and Raven, "Bases of Social Power," 154.
9. French and Raven, "Bases of Social Power," 155.
10. French and Raven, "Bases of Social Power," 155.
11. French and Raven, "Bases of Social Power," 155.

power in this way: expert power depends on my credibility, while informational power depends on how I communicate, e.g., my use of logic, facts, empathy, deception, etc. The con artist doctor may rely on informational power to hide her lack of actual expertise. In this way informational power and expert power are distinct, but may well describe the same act of power.

Legitimate power: My established right to influence you coupled with your established obligation to accept my influence.[12] This is the power a referee has to call a technical foul on a coach, and the power an army major has to give orders to a private.

The question quickly becomes: How was this right established? Who gave you the authority? This question has several answers, e.g., socially established structures and designation from others with legitimate power.[13]

Social norms and cultural values can also be sources of legitimate power.[14] For example, when I see a person slip on the ice and say to myself, "I cannot just walk by and not help," I am responding to the *legitimate power of dependence*.[15] This is an informal but strongly felt obligation to help someone in need of assistance, based on the cultural values instilled in me.

Legitimate position power[16] is granted along with formal roles like school principal and police officer.

Raven and French argue that the use of legitimate power is, in some instances, undergirded by formal coercive power, i.e., "the legitimate right to threaten punishment for nonconformity."[17] A judge has the formal, given authority to issue a bench warrant for arrest. The police officer has the legitimate power to use deadly force if she deems it necessary in the moment.

---

12. French and Raven, "Bases of Social Power," 153.
13. French and Raven, "Bases of Social Power," 153.
14. Pierro, et al., "Bases of Social Power," 3.
15. Pierro, et al., "Bases of Social Power," 3.
16. Pierro, et al., "Bases of Social Power," 3.
17. French and Raven, "Bases of Social Power," 154.

Section 1: Ingredients of Power

French: Harsh versus Soft Power

Bertram French researched and refined these power bases over the following decades. He and his colleagues further differentiated them into the practical, informative forms of *harsh* and *soft power*. "Harsh power bases, as the name suggests, constrain individuals' freedom to comply with the leader's demands."[18] Harsh power bases include coercion, reward, and legitimate position power. Those influenced by these forms of power have limited options for how to respond.

Soft power bases, such as expert, referent, and informational power, "endow organizational members with more freedom and autonomy in accepting the demands of the influencing agent."[19] I am free to take or leave these forms of influence, or respond at a later time, or in a specific form I choose.

THE CARROT AND THE STICK: TRUST-BASED AND DISTRUST-BASED POWER

Power can be distinguished according to those forms founded on some level of trust, and those founded on some level of distrust.

Some forms of power, such as reward power, referent power, and expert power, are "based on trust."[20] Do I trust your expert advice about the stock market, and invest accordingly? Do I believe you when you tell me this used car is a good buy? By trusting you, I am choosing to place my dependence on you, i.e., to give you power.

Trust-based power can be based on deception. As long as you believe me, I can pass myself off as an expert on Beethoven or as a successful businessman. An online misinformation campaign that seeks to sway voters to a particular candidate, or to not vote, is relying on trust-based power.

Some forms of power are *distrust-based*, or coercive. The state trooper, for example, has the power to punish me by ticketing me in

---

18. Pierro, et al., "Bases of Social Power," 3.
19. Pierro, et al., "Bases of Social Power," 3.
20. Coleman, "Power and Conflict," 3rd ed., 152–53

order to achieve her desired outcome of traffic safety. A government agency may publicly fine a corporation for fraud, in part to deter other corporations from doing the same thing.

The connection between trust, distrust, and power will be explored further in chapter 10, in part by differentiating both trust and distrust in *calculus-based* and *identification-based* forms.

THE CARROT *AND* THE STICK: AL CAPONE

> *You can get much farther with a kind word and a gun than you can with a kind word alone.*
> —Al Capone

Al Capone demonstrates the common reality that power roles, especially given authority roles, are often a blend of both trust-based and distrust-based power. A basketball coach may be revered for the skills he instills and his knowledge of the game, but also have the legitimate, distrust-based power to bench a player for breaking team rules. A math teacher may know her subject (expertise), and how to teach it (informational power), and have a strong rapport with her students (interpersonal linkage power), but still use her authority to send a tardy student to the office (formal distrust-based power).

In the carrot-and-stick metaphor, stick-related (coercive) questions are:

- Do you actually have a stick?
- Will you actually use the stick?
- Will the stick hurt?
- Who else has a stick?

   Carrot-related (trust-based) questions include:

- Can you provide the carrot?
- Will you provide the carrot?
- Do I want the carrot?

SECTION 1: INGREDIENTS OF POWER

- Can I get a carrot in other ways?
- Does someone else have a better carrot?

CONVERTING THE CARROT TO A STICK

Any form of power can be converted to coercive power, by simply withholding it, or threatening to. A wealthy donor to a museum, for example, may threaten to withhold her traditional annual gift if a certain controversial traveling exhibition is scheduled. Trade union members may engage in a slow-down strike, performing their specialized duties but at half the production level until terms are reached.

Two ironies present themselves when converting trust-based to distrust-based power. First, converting trust-based power to coercive power may be more effective, i.e., more powerful, than that form of power in its original, trust-based form. The power of the rich donor, for example, may be felt more tangibly by her threatening to withhold money than by giving it.

A second irony: using a trust-based form of power coercively is often much simpler and easier than using that form of power in its original form. To force a new contract, for example, the hold-out basketball player simply stops doing the physically demanding, dangerous work he is valued for doing. The trade union members are not as fatigued by their slower pace.

The fact that any form of power can easily be converted to coercive power, coupled with how common this step is, and how unsettling it is to surrounding relationships, contribute to why power is often equated with adversarial dynamics like coercion and manipulation.

One Act of Power, Many Lenses

Different forms of power can be employed at the same time. A child may say "pretty please" and offer a cute smile to persuade Gramma to buy her a candy bar, while both know a loud in-store temper tantrum is her immediate Plan B. The child's use of informational power, reward power, and threatened coercive power may easily override Gramma's legitimate power and resource control power.

Further, the same act of power may be described differently by a high-power party than it is by a low-power party. The company president may say to a regional manager, "I'm hoping you can do me a favor." The request may be worded and stated as a soft-power request. But to the regional manager this may well be heard as a coercive, non-negotiable, harsh-power command.

The ability to describe certain acts of power according to these types—resource control, informational power, trust-based, soft, harsh, etc.—is helpful. But it may be more helpful to be able to:

- assess any act of power through multiple lenses,
- recognize what overlapping forms of power are in play at once,
- recognize how the same act of power can be seen as coercive by one party and collaborative by another.

However, while the same act of power can be described according to multiple currencies and bases, Raven and French provide studied means to distinguish certain power bases in some instances. Consider two important examples:

- Coercive power and reward power can appear to be two sides of the same coin, i.e., not being punished can be considered a reward. Which is which becomes the choice of the person being influenced. And that choice manifests itself in *attraction* or *dependence*. Specifically, perceived use of reward power will increase attraction, whereas perceived use of coercive power will decrease it. Also, coercive power requires dependence, and requires that dependence be maintained or increased as needed for that coercive power to remain effective. Raven and French specify that reward power doesn't rely on dependence.[21]

- Referent power offers a clear platform for both reward and coercive power. However, Raven and French offer an intriguing

21. French and Raven, "Bases of Social Power," 152–53.

means to distinguish referent power by clarifying the source of coercion and reward. Do you punish me or do I punish myself? If *you* punish me for not meeting your requirements, that is coercive power. However, if *I* punish myself for not meeting your requirements, that is sign I am influenced by your referent power.[22]

SETTING-BASED POWER: ECOLOGICAL, NORMATIVE, AND DESIGNATED

As Coleman and others remind us, "power is context-dependent."[23] Some forms of power, however, establish that context. *Ecological*, *designated*, and *normative* power are best understood by describing how they help construct the platform upon which other social power dynamics function.

Ecological Power

This form of power sets the stage upon which other forms of power are determined within the group. This is the power to, for example, construct a courtroom so that the judge is elevated above everyone else, to dress the judge in imposing black robes, and to command "all rise" when the judge enters the courtroom. This setting-defining power "entails sufficient control over the other's social or physical environment to permit one to modify it so that the modified environment induces the desired behavior or prevents undesired behavior."[24] Ecological power is the power to control group processes, such as when a board chairman places a controversial item at the bottom of the agenda to limit discussion. Prisons are monuments to ecological power, built with walls, razor wire fences, and furniture fastened to the floor. A prison warden may also use other forms of ecological power, such as giving inmates pants that are

---

22. French and Raven, "Bases of Social Power," 154.
23. Coleman, "Power and Conflict," 1st. ed., 124.
24. Deutsch, *Resolution of Conflict*, 88.

much too large and no belts, requiring them to hold their pants up while standing. This simple step occupies their hands and hinders them in the event of a fight.

Primary or Normative Power

Primary power, also called *normative power*, is the power to define *normal* and *right*.

> *Primary power is "the ability to affect those activities (e.g. the law, the media, policies) that define a domain. This includes what is considered 'good' in a society: prosocial versus antisocial forms of violence (e.g. 'freedom fighter' versus 'terrorism'), morality, religion, ideology, politics, education, and so on."*[25]

What does the group believe, and what norms will individuals adhere to, as part of that group? This is the power the group has on the individuals who value belonging to it, and want to be accepted within it.

Formal declarations of normative power include Semper Fi, the Pledge of Allegiance, the HP Way, and the Cadet Honor Code. These examples formally state what behaviors and attitudes should be seen as virtuous and, explicitly or implicitly, what is deviant. Informal forms of normative power include initiation rites, hazing, pecking order, and peer pressure.

Normative power "is based on the obligations that the other has to accept one's influence as a result of social norms governing the relationship."[26] Normative power is the often quiet power used to maintain homeostasis in a group. Individuals exerting primary power are also making bids for ownership of the setting. Normative power is heard in power-bid statements like:

- "You'll need to learn the ropes."
- "We need preserve our way of life."

---

25. Coleman, "Power and Conflict," 3rd. ed., 141.
26. Deutsch, *Resolution of Conflict*, 87.

Section 1: Ingredients of Power

- "Don't step out of line."
- "You should go back where you belong."
- "Wait until things get back to normal."
- "That's how we've always done it around here."

The connection between normative power and resistance can be appreciated by revisiting Senge's concept of balancing processes:

> *Whenever there is "resistance to change," you can count on their being one or more "hidden" balancing processes. Resistance to change is neither capricious nor mysterious. It almost always arises from threats to traditional norms and ways of doing things. Often these norms are woven into the fabric of established power relationships.*[27]

Designated Power

Designated power is the most recognizable form of power. "The President of the United States, police officers, managers at work, and professors all have certain designations of power in a particular role."[28] As private individuals, we designate legitimate power to the employers, coaches, and teachers. By tradition, societies down through history have designated power to certain people due to gender, royal lineage, age, height, land ownership, etc. Those with designated power enforce the rules we live by and want others to live by. In this way normative power, ecological power, and designated power complement each other, to the point of being different sides of the same coin.

Another reason designated power is easily recognized is because it *wants* to be. Police officers drive vehicles with vividly contrasting colors, flashing lights, and loud sirens precisely to be noticed. Referees wear striped shirts and blow loud whistles. Generals wear shiny stars on their collars. These symbols of designated power are meant to be quickly understood. Everyone knows at a

---

27. Senge, *Fifth Discipline*, 88.
28. Hocker and Wilmot, *Interpersonal Power*, 119.

glance who is in charge. Similarly, we designate power to bright symbolic objects like stoplights, yellow lines on the road, and handicapped parking signs.

Further, these designated symbols can communicate power from great distance, with varying effects. Consider the range of strong responses to a police uniform: "The psychological and physical impact of the police uniform should not be underestimated. Depending on the background of the citizen, the police uniform can elicit emotions ranging from pride and respect, to fear and anger."[29] A police uniform, even from blocks away, can communicate trust-based power to me and dangerously coercive power to you.

Power-Distance Cultures—Hofstede

When Peter Drucker said, "Culture eats strategy for breakfast," he was describing the reality-defining, collective identity-defining influence of setting-based power. Another way to grasp the profound depth of setting-based power is to consider the terms we use when attempting to confront it: revolution, rebellion, uprising, revolt, mutiny, coup, insurrection. This setting-defining blend of ecological, normative and designated power is also illustrated in Geert Hofstede's studies of power-distance cultures.

Hofstede defines power-distance as "the extent to which the less powerful members of institutions and organizations within a country expect and accept that power is distributed unequally."[30] Some settings are low power-distance, meaning those within them are more likely to question authority, and view power imbalance with apprehension.

Hofstede's analysis has led him to designate countries like India, Bangladesh, and China as large power-distance cultures: people within these settings are more likely to "accept a hierarchical order in which everybody has a place and which needs no further justification." By contrast, in small power-distance cultures, like Canada and Austria, power imbalance is more likely to be met with anxiety

29. Johnson, "Psychological Influence of the Police Uniform."
30. Hofstede Center, "Power Distance Dimensions."

and efforts to balance power. "In societies with low power distance, people strive to equalize the distribution of power and demand justification for inequalities of power."[31]

These cultures differ greatly in how they view authority. Those within large power-distance cultures accept power imbalance as appropriate. "Hierarchy in [such] an organization is seen as reflecting inherent inequalities, centralization is popular, subordinates expect to be told what to do and the ideal boss is a benevolent autocrat." Meanwhile, those in small power-distance cultures see authority as necessary but meriting accountability. "Hierarchy is established for convenience, superiors are always accessible and managers rely on individual employees and teams for their expertise."[32]

Ting-Toomey and Chung describe how large power-distance cultures differ from small power-distance cultures in approach to education and family. "In large power distance family situations, children are expected to obey their parents. Children are punished if they talk back or contradict their parents." In small power-distance settings, "children may contradict their parents and speak their mind. They are expected to show self-initiative and learn verbal articulateness and persuasion skills."[33] Ting-Toomey and Chung also describe how in large power-distance settings teachers are likely to lecture, while in small power-distance settings teachers are more likely to discuss and ask for feedback.[34]

GLOBAL SURVIVAL: POWER VERSUS INFLUENCE

Influence differs from power. Morton Deutsch, perhaps the leading scholarly authority on power, makes the important distinction that "power is deliberate or purposive influence." Influence by itself can be unintentional, encompassing unwanted consequences. The

---

31. Hofstede Center, "Power Distance Dimensions."
32. Hofstede Center, "Power Distance Dimensions."
33. Ting-Toomey and Chung, *Understanding Intercultural Communication*, 64–65.
34. Ting-Toomey and Chung, *Understanding Intercultural Communication*, 64–65.

author recalls a dad-to-be stating that "the kind of father I am going to be will be my revenge against my own father." The first father's negative impact on his son (and indirect positive impact on his grandchild) were factors of his influence, not his power. Consider four other varied examples of unintended influence:

- In September 1928, Dr. Alexander Fleming left an open petri dish containing staphylococcal bacteria near an open window in his lab. Mold spores, likely floating into the lab through the window, landed in the petri dish. Fleming found that the mold spores had killed the bacteria. In short, a messy laboratory led to the discovery of penicillin. In 1945, Fleming was awarded the Nobel Prize for his mistake. He later said, "One sometimes finds, what one is not looking for. When I woke up just after dawn on September 28, 1928, I certainly didn't plan to revolutionize all medicine by discovering the world's first antibiotic, or bacteria killer. But I suppose that was exactly what I did."[35]

- In November 2019 a dying juvenile sperm whale became stranded on Seilebost Beach on the Scottish Isle of Harris. A necropsy removed a "huge ball" of plastic trash—weighing 220 pounds—from its stomach.

- In the 800,000 years prior to 1950, carbon dioxide levels in the Earth's atmosphere had never gone above 300 parts per million. In the last 70 years, this number has risen to over 400 parts per million.

- Clara Belle Williams graduated in 1937, at age 51, from New Mexico State University with a degree in English. However, she was not allowed to participate in the graduation ceremony because she was black. Because of her skin color she was not allowed inside classrooms, so she took notes while sitting outside in the hall. In 2005, twelve years after her death, NMSU renamed its English department after her.

For worse or better, my influence can lead to ends I did not foresee. Noteworthy about the above examples: the encouraging

---

35. Tan and Tatsumura, "Alexander Fleming," 366.

Section 1: Ingredients of Power

stories all involve the influence of individuals, where the troubling stories all demonstrate societal-level influence.

When Andy Crouch and Dacher Keltner define power according to one's ability "to make a difference in the world," this merits important qualification. These definitions, along with others that do not expressly state intentionality, serve also as definitions of influence.

Much evidence declares that we can influence, unintentionally, devastating changes in our world. It is quite possible that human influence will put an end to all power, social and individual, human and beyond. We will survive, and ideally thrive, only if our power overcomes our influence.

4
An Every-Person Appreciation of Power

Heroes need monsters to establish their heroic credentials. You need something scary to overcome.
—Margaret Atwood

What we need is a system of thought—you might even call it a religion—that can bind humans together.
—Abraham Maslow

We buy things we don't need with money we don't have to impress people we don't like.
—Chuck Palahniuk, *Fight Club*

All you need in this life is ignorance and confidence, and then success is sure.
—Mark Twain

Maslow's hierarchy of needs is often displayed graphically as a layered pyramid. It serves as a stable, enduring monument to every person's constant, multifaceted need for power. Maslow categorizes human needs into five levels:

Section 1: Ingredients of Power

- Level 5—Self-actualization needs: self-fulfillment, self-awareness, creativity
- Level 4—Esteem needs: accomplishment, recognition
- Level 3—Belonging needs: friends, relationships, intimacy
- Level 2—Safety needs: security, shelter from harm
- Level 1—Physiological needs: food, water, warmth, rest

Our most basic survival needs reside at the bottom. Self-actualization needs, considered the most ideal and difficult to attain, are at the top. These levels, and the needs listed within each one, have long been subject to debate and modification. But the structure itself withstands the test of time.

The value of Maslow's hierarchy in a discussion of power is twofold. First, it succinctly illustrates every being's constant, unending need for power. Second, it efficiently contrasts the widely varying reasons we need power. All the elements within all these levels require some form of power, individual or social.

Something to be noted here about Maslow's hierarchy, and explored further in chapter 9:

- Those needs associated with the first two levels can, if necessary, be attained by individual power.
- Needs in levels 3 and 4 are met primarily through social power, with few exceptions. Others must help us meet our needs for respect, belonging, intimacy, etc.
- Needs associated with the top-most level, self-actualization, are met only through individual power. I must attain these myself, independently of others.

An Every-Person Appreciation of Power

MYRIAD NEEDS AND WANTS FOR POWER

Consider the following list. Each item constitutes either a desired outcome or the impetus for one. Many require influencing other people. Each and all shape a person's need for power.

wants	expectations	purposes	concerns	respect
needs	interests	motivations	health	notice
promises	objectives	hopes	hope	dignity
family	impulses	lusts	anxiety	belonging
values	satisfaction	independence	envy	reputation
love	preferences	empathy	addictions	honor
thirst	freedom	obligations	money	validation
peace	temptations	convenience	meaning	esteem
safety	longing	entertainment	urges	affirmation
fatigue	intimacy	orders	intentions	acceptance
hunger	desires	responsibilities	belongings	approval

This list could be much longer and still incomplete, especially if it listed needs and wants more specifically: warm clothing, safe drinking water, protein. Who is not managing dozens of items in this table at the same time?

Several of the items listed merit careful consideration relative to power:

- Many of these goals—hopes, temptations, thirst—have at least some measure of power *over* me.

- Those goals that involve relationships—e.g., respect, belonging, esteem—require social power. I must influence others to gain these.

- Additionally, those goals that involve relationships—e.g., esteem, validation, responsibilities—give others power over me. What power do I give others due to my need for affirmation and approval?

Further, many items listed compete. How constantly do my work responsibilities interfere with my family obligations? How easily do my immediate cravings, say for fast food and beer, win out over my long-term ideals like health and ideal BMI?

Which column of previous table causes me greater concern—the first or the last? Returning to Maslow's heirarchy, the needs listed in the last column reside on Maslow's third and second levels. None rises to the first level: self-actualization. Others may debate whether these form a foundation to reach Maslow's highest level. Nevertheless, these terms help clarify that highest level by contrasting it.

What is self-actualization? Who am I by myself, actually, apart from the validation of others? How do I choose to honor myself even if no-one else honors me? What about me do I approve of even if others don't affirm that? Do I find joy in what I've created, even if others don't notice it?

My answers to questions like these help determine my individual power and my need for social power. Do I need the approval and acceptance of others more than I need those things from myself?

Prospective and Transactive Goals

I recognize some goals or ambitions or duties in a *prospective* way, i.e., well before my efforts to achieve them. A college graduate may have a five-year-plan that includes applying to law school. A kindergartner may want to be a firefighter when they grow up.

My goals and concerns may also be *transactive*. I may sense them only in the moment, only in response to some stimulus as you and I interact. I may become concerned about my boundaries or my rights only after they have been violated. Transactive concerns may come as a surprise. I may, for example, realize my need for respect only when I feel I have been disrespected.

DIFFERENTIATING TYPES OF GOALS

Just as definitions of power can be differentiated, and specific forms of power can be differentiated, the specific goals we need power to attain can be differentiated. Interpersonal conflict scholars Hocker and Wilmot describe four kinds of goals we bring into relationships, and

An Every-Person Appreciation of Power

hence into the conflicts within those relationships.[1] Understanding these goals helps clarify my specific needs around power:

Outcome goals focus on the task or tasks we depend on each other to accomplish. We may have a *mutual outcome* we are working on together, such as a software engineering team working toward a go-live date. Or we may be seeking to accomplish *complimentary* outcomes. You, for example, may want to buy a gallon of paint and my store wants to sell you one, and employs me to help you make the purchase. Outcome goals understandably correspond with *outcome emphasis* definitions of power.

Relational goals focus on who we want to be to each other. How closely do I want to associate with you? An example of contrasting relationship goals in a professional setting: you want to be my exclusive parts provider, where I prefer the freedom to work with several suppliers. On a personal level, how do my relational goals as an introvert differ from yours as an extrovert? Relational goals change as settings change, even within the same relationship. I may like working with you, but not like driving to work with you because you read all the street signs out loud. You may enjoy my friendship, but shudder at the idea of raising children with me.

Where task goals are often tangible and easily described, relational goals can be harder to identify and describe, and more awkward to discuss. How do you, for example, maintain an important professional relationship with me even as I hint at wanting to be more than friends?

Process goals are those means a group uses to maintain itself, make decisions, and define the goals it seeks to achieve. Does the board vote on a new initiative as a whole, or provide input before the chairperson decides? On a national scale, elections are processes, as is the overall system of checks and balances. When four friends approach a car and one yells "shotgun," this is a sacred process, influenced by the movie *The Magnificent Seven*, to reserve the front passenger seat.

Identity goals include my need for respect, admiration, validation, belonging, etc. How do I want to be regarded? Do you see

---

1. Hocker and Wilmot, *Interpersonal Conflict*, 10th ed., 77.

Section 1: Ingredients of Power

me as an equal? How do others in my community regard me, my beliefs, my values, my gender, my skin color, my intelligence?

My *prospective identity goals* include my ambitions, ideals, beliefs, hopes, and desire for belonging. I am aware of these long before I enter any relationships and negotiate social power. I may dream of fulfilling some identity goals, like being famous, since early in childhood.

Face concerns, or *transactive identity concerns*, are those identity concerns I feel in the moments a specific interaction is unfolding. "Face is something that is emotionally invested, and that can be lost, maintained, or enhanced, and must be constantly attended to in interaction."[2] Do I feel respected as we are speaking? Are you using a dismissive tone of voice? Did you just call me "boy" when you cut me off mid-sentence? Questions like these illustrate the immediate importance of face concerns.

IDENTITY IS EVERYTHING

> *Image is everything.*
> —Andre Agassi

Concerns around identity and face may well drive our most intense needs for power. For example, *prospective identity goals*—e.g., ambitions, values, desire for recognition—pivotally determine other outcome goals and relationship goals I value. Meanwhile, face concerns encompass my in-the-moment identity needs. To appreciate the crucial importance of face concerns, consider just some of the terms used when someone experiences *face loss*. If I lose face I may feel insulted, offended, demeaned, humiliated, invalidated, disrespected, dishonored, or rejected.

My identity as a whole is understood better by understanding the differences between my personal identity, social identity, shared identity, collective identity, and institutional identity. These intermingled *facets of identity* will be explored in chapter 9. *Positive face* will also be defined and distinguished from *negative face* in that chapter.

---

2. Brown and Levinson, *Politeness*, 61.

AN EVERY-PERSON APPRECIATION OF POWER

How Goals Intertwine in the Moment

Outcome, relationship, process, identity, and face goals impact each other constantly. A single ambition may simultaneously create ongoing outcome, relationship, and identity goals, and prompt specific face concerns as I interact. A professor of political science may simultaneously seek to educate (outcome), engage her students deeply as she teaches (relationship), and prefer her students call her Professor when they address her (identity and face). Her title itself is a fleeting but indelible act of power. In as little as one word, a title:

- defines the relationship,
- defines the outcomes that relationship exists to achieve,
- describes the process by which those outcomes will be achieved,
- indicates prospective and transactive identity concerns,
- suggests several different forms of authority.

EXPECTATIONS: HOW YOUR POWER BECOMES MINE

We use many familiar terms to describe the state in which one party's power is transferred to another:

assumptions	obligations	expectations	responsibilities
promises	requirements	commitments	agreements
contracts	arrangements	duties	requests
deals	bargains	assurances	favors
commands	delegation	given authority	pacts

Each of these names a relationship threshold in which my power becomes devoted to achieve your objectives. Some of these arrangements are entered into more easily and informally than others. A contract, for example, may involve multiple signatures including by a notary public. On the other end of the spectrum, an assumption or expectation may form without words or even

Section 1: Ingredients of Power

awareness. You may not even know of your responsibility until you have failed to meet it. Did you forget to pick up my dry-cleaning this week? With each of dynamics, I gain power by obligating your power. Your power becomes mine.

5

An Every-Moment Awareness of Power

Between stimulus and response there is space. In that space is our power to choose our response. In our response lies our growth and our freedom.
    —Victor Frankl, *Man's Search for Meaning*

Jacob Philadelphia could have been much more nervous. Yes, his dad, who worked at the White House, had told him the person standing before him was the President of the United States. And yes, they were standing in the Oval Office. But at five years old, Jacob didn't really grasp the significance.

"I thought that he didn't have that much power, he was just an ordinary person," Jacob would recall later.[1]

Still, Jacob was uneasy, and spoke so quietly, according to the *New York Times*, that the President had to make him repeat his request.

"I want to know if my hair is just like yours," he said.

"Why don't you touch it and see for yourself?"

And the President bent over low, so Jacob could reach his head.

"Touch it, dude!"

"So, what do you think?"

---

1. Hathaway, "Boy in Touching Obama Photo."

Section 1: Ingredients of Power

"Yes, it does feel the same."

Nothing about this interaction between Jacob Philadelphia and President Barack Obama is *not* about power. Power inhabits every interaction between people. "Just as we cannot not communicate, we cannot not use power."[2] "We are constantly influencing the behavior of others and likewise being influenced by them."[3]

If two male strangers pass each other in a narrow hallway, they may instinctively catch one another's eye and nod their heads slightly, both as a greeting and as way of assuring *I mean you no harm*. No words are exchanged and perhaps only a second elapses, but both parties deliberately influence each other, and important purposes are achieved.

In a stark contrast, a young female passing a male stranger in the same hallway may well look down and avoid eye contact, for a number of reasons. First, she may not want to *send the wrong message*. Second, she may not want to receive any number of *relational messages* that may come within such a look. "Relationships are defined and redefined with every message that speakers send. As a result, relational moves are second nature."[4] "While most people dislike discussions of their own power, one cannot avoid using power."[5]

SIT DOWN: POWER AS PARAVERBAL, NONVERBAL, AND PROXEMIC

Understanding how power impacts all interactions requires understanding the different levels on which we communicate. Consider the example of one person saying to another, "Sit down." On a *report* or *information level*, this statement has one meaning. The informational level conveys spoken words and their most commonly understood meanings.

But how many different ways can these words be stated on the *relational* or *command level*? On a command level, "sit down" can

---

2. Hocker and Wilmot, *Interpersonal Conflict*, 96.
3. Steinke, *How Your Church Family Works*, 121
4. Folger et al., *Working Through Conflict*, 155.
5. Hocker and Wilmot, *Interpersonal Conflict*, 96.

An Every-Moment Awareness of Power

be stated as a terse order from a superior, or as a host's plea to *let me honor you by serving you.*

Each different way this message can be spoken constitutes a unique negotiation of power. "Relational messages are always bids [for power]. They attempt to define a certain type of relationship. But they may or may not be successful depending on the listener's response."[6] How I respond to your bid for power is my own bid for power. "During any face-to-face interaction, people constantly define and redefine their relationship."[7]

Many command-level messages are communicated on the *paraverbal level*. Paraverbal messaging includes tone, pace, volume, and inflection in how words are spoken. With the same two spoken words, these can combine to give entirely different commands on a relational level.

Nonverbal messaging is often called body language. Examples of nonverbal messaging can include shoulder position, use of open-handed gestures, or just plain pointing at the other person's nose. And how much is communicated when the other person responds nonverbally, perhaps by rolling her eyes, or giving a heavy sigh before responding? Wordless gestures—steady eye contact or furrowing one's brow—can speak volumes. The statement "If looks could kill, he'd be dead right now," though hyperbole, speaks to the power of nonverbal communication.

Proxemics is nonverbal communication through the use of space. Do I move close to you when telling you what I want, threatening you by taking up your personal space? Do I make way for you when we pass in the hall, or do I *barge through*, expecting you to accommodate me? When President Obama bent down close to Jacob Philadelphia's face, practically forcing him to touch his head, this was an intensely validating use of proxemics.

What we communicate on nonverbal and paraverbal levels is generally considered more believable and compelling, i.e., more powerful, than what we actually say. *Actions speak louder than words.* One of the simplest forms of passive-aggressive manipulation is to

---

6. Folger et al., *Working Through Conflict*, 154.
7. Folger et al., *Working Through Conflict*, 154.

Section 1: Ingredients of Power

make one statement on a report level—*I'm fine!*—and communicate the opposite on a paraverbal, relational level.

TEXT AND EMAIL: MODERATING RELATIONAL MESSAGES

Given these dual, sometimes dueling levels on which we communicate during any in-person interaction, the growing preference for written communication—texts and emails—only makes sense. These methods of communication greatly reduce relational-level messaging. Interpreting the power dynamics in a reply text message, for example, may be limited to assessing the choice of words used and how quickly the reply was sent.

Compared with face-to-face communication, a text message slows down the interaction. A response text may come hours later without causing concern. A text message also minimizes relational level messaging, largely removing proxemics and paraverbal communication.

Texting and emailing are simply less relationally complex, i.e., less stressful. Still, written communication is itself mysterious and subject to misinterpretation. Does the ellipsis at the end of a text message indicate impatience or just a passing thought?

SERIOUSLY BUT NOT LITERALLY: POWER/NO-POWER BIDS

Many familiar statements can be classified as *power/no-power bids*:

- "I was just joking around."
- "I was drunk when I said that."
- "Did you think I was serious?"
- "That was locker-room talk."
- "I was just teasing."
- "Forget what I said."

An Every-Moment Awareness of Power

The above statements all attempt to negate or modify a prior bid for power. These are information level bids to redefine the relationship, and specify the power I want to exert within it now. Power/no-power bids can be subtly but keenly coercive, as will be described in chapter 9.

SHARING AND UNSHARING POWER

Power can be shared, such as when one traveler who speaks Italian teaches others in the group how to say "train station," or when the child with the only baseball bat allows other players to use it. But these differing examples illustrate the consequences of sharing different forms of power. When the child shares the bat, for example, this form of resource control power can be taken back. In contrast, whatever expertise or special skills the traveler shares are forms of power that cannot be unshared.

SECTION 2

Power in Context

6

Endorsement: Negotiating Power

In systems thinking it is an axiom that every influence is both cause and effect. Nothing is ever influenced in just one direction.

—Peter Senge[1]

Power is never the property of an individual; it belongs to a group and remains in existence only so long as the group keeps together.

—Hannah Arendt[2]

Being powerful is like being a lady. If you have to tell people you are, you aren't.

—Margaret Thatcher

Individual power should not be mistaken for social power; the latter differs fundamentally from the former. My individual power is my ability to achieve a desired objective by myself. What outcome, process or identity goals can I achieve on my own? Your social power is your ability to influence others to achieve an objective you desire. What identity goals, e.g., belonging, acceptance, admiration, can

---

1. Senge, *Fifth Discipline*, 75.
2. Arendt, *On Violence*, 44.

be achieved only within relationship? Whereas individuals *possess* individual power, "[social] power is the property of the relationship rather than the quality of the individual."[3]

Familiar phrases like "Michelle has a lot of power in the math department" and "Senator Talbert has the most influence on the committee" are misleading. They adhere to a misperception "that power flows in one direction (usually from the top down) and that individuals with differing levels of power do not mutually influence each other."[4] "Many theorists who have been concerned with power have focused on it solely as an attribute of the actor. This neglects its relational aspects and implicitly assumes that it remains constant across situations, an assumption that is clearly false."[5] A person can have immense social power one moment, and little to none the next, depending on how the context changes.

POWER DEPENDS ON ENDORSEMENT

Social power is subject to constant negotiation. Folger, Poole, and Stutman encapsulate this ongoing process in the term *endorsement*. "If power stems from relationships, it is misleading to try to identify a particular person who holds power. The more important question may be who assents to the use of power or who withholds endorsement."[6]

Endorsement can take place quickly or slowly, verbally or nonverbally, formally or informally. Endorsement may be specific and immediate, such as a Marine private stating, "Sir, yes, sir," in response to an officer's command. An audience giving a standing ovation at the end of a performance is a clear but nonverbal sign of endorsement.

Endorsement is often confirmed entirely on the relational level. The Marine private actually following orders after the officer leaves is the true endorsement of the officer's power. When another

---

3. Hocker and Wilmot, *Interpersonal Conflict*, 9th ed., 116.
4. Coleman, *"Power and Conflict,"* 1st ed., 112.
5. Deutsch, *Resolution of Conflict*, 85.
6. Folger et al., *Working Through Conflict*, 166.

Endorsement: Negotiating Power

person is speaking, simply not interrupting endorses that person's power. Rosa Parks's decision to not move from her seat was a long, silent refusal to endorse power.

Endorsement also looks like not doing something I want to do when another person calls for restraint. A teenager endorses his mother's power by resisting the urge to rummage through the fridge because she has told him not to snack right before dinner. In this way, restraint can be at once a display of individual power and an endorsement of another's social power.

ENDORSEMENT IS CONSTANTLY NEGOTIATED

Any single act of endorsement occupies just one specific point in an ongoing process. Motorists may slow down for a known speed trap, but return to exceeding the speed limit for the rest of their commute. A child who cleaned his room obediently at age six may need to be admonished to do so at eleven.

To help appreciate the nuanced complexity of endorsement process as it plays out, individually, in the moment, consider the following simple setting:

> A group of twenty or so has gathered to help their friend Doug move out of his apartment. Anne Marie climbs up into the back of the rental truck, and turns to face the others. She declares confidently that she has moved three times before and she's an authority on how to load moving trucks. She instructs the group to bring her the heavy boxes first.

Anne Marie's power is far from established at this point. She does not *have* power by just proclaiming expertise and then giving instructions. In fact, her most power-establishing step may instead be the proxemic act of placing herself in the truck. Myriad endorsement-related responses are reasonable. What range of responses—internal, expressed, emotional, face-related—might her specific bid for power illicit at this moment?

- Some may head off to find heavy boxes because they trust her confidence and expertise. Others endorse her clarity and head off as well.

- Someone may *negotiate endorsement,* asking, "Shouldn't we load the refrigerator first?"

- Someone else may ask almost the same question, but in a significantly different way: "Shouldn't we bring you the refrigerator first?" This response endorses her legitimate power specifically: she's in charge. But it negotiates endorsement of her expert power. "Shouldn't we do this differently?" This question also negotiates Anne Marie's power to determine process goals.

- Someone may *withhold* endorsement of Anne Marie's bid for power, saying, "Tell us your plan first."

- Someone else may say, "I like you, Anne Marie, but that's not the right way to do it." This response attempts to steward her identity, but denies endorsement of her expertise and authority.

- Others may just bring out whatever they find first and set it down near the truck. This partially endorses Anne Marie's power by accommodating it, while still furthering the group's task.

- Others (Doug has many friends and much stuff) may simply not hear what she said. She failed to get their attention, a separate act of power and endorsement.

- Two movers may calmly endorse Anne Marie's bid for power by doing exactly as she says, but not because of her clarity, expertise, or charisma. They don't care who loads the truck, how, or how well. They're just happy to not have that job for the tenth time.

Anne Marie's one bid for power, her eight-second effort to initiate *deliberate influence,* prompts numerous endorsement-related responses. Each person she attempts to influence will negotiate endorsement uniquely, and set off more power-related dynamics by doing so. Some of these will be obvious, some undetectable, some verbal, some silent. Further, each person's endorsement of her power has as much to do with their own goals as it does with her bid.

ONGOING ENDORSEMENT

The above example of moving day is limited in key ways. The group is assembled for one specific, immediate task, and it's made up of volunteers. The group will disband within in a few hours. Other settings in which power dynamics play out are ongoing—e.g., the regional office of a multinational oil company, the Republican National Committee, a nursing home—with more complex task, process, relationship, and identity goals.

How might the endorsement process look in a formally established, ongoing setting? Suppose Anne Marie is the morning shift manager at an inbound call center. Everyone she manages is paid; they depend on this setting for their rent, car payment, and groceries. Will Anne Marie's job be easier now? Will process changes—e.g., "All employees must work from the office wearing an approved mask"— meet with no resistance? Will everyone just do as they're told? In short, will Anne Marie's power no longer be subject to endorsement?

Consider another setting: Anne Marie is a sorority president, with dozens of members, pledges, and other officers around her. This group exists not to accomplish a joint task, but instead to further their personal, social and collective identity goals. Instead of being paid for their work, or voluntarily participating, members pay dues to belong to this group. Is the power that comes with Anne Marie's role still subject to endorsement? If she gives an order—say, introducing a new, more strict and modest on-campus dress code—how will her sorority respond? By what means will they negotiate endorsement of her power in the moments, minutes, hours, days, and weeks to follow?

ENDORSEMENT IS INSTINCTIVE

Just like power is a subtle factor in every interpersonal interaction, so is the endorsement of power. Endorsement is often instinctive, such as when someone behind me says "pardon me" and I quickly move to the left or right. "The tendency to endorse power is deep-seated and based in powerful and pervasive social processes. At the most superficial level, we endorse power because the resources it is based on enable others to grant or deny things that are valuable."[7]

One person may endorse another as a careful, conscious choice, such as voting for a specific candidate. Or we may grant someone power based solely on appearances or first impression. I may assume a person wearing glasses is smart and bookish, or that a muscular person is a talented athlete. "We endorse those we expect to be powerful and do not endorse those we expect to be weak."[8] "The tendency and willingness to endorse power stems from several sources, including preconceptions about what makes a person weak or strong, an aura of mystery, and the judicial use of authority, and evidence of valued skills or abilities."[9]

ENDORSEMENT: MORE POWERFUL THAN POWER

Consider some of the specific, practical ways in which the endorsement of power can be as or more powerful than power itself:

- Withholding endorsement can itself be a source of power. Senator Talbert's colleague can simply refrain from committing to vote in favor of his proposed bill, perhaps to gain concessions she wants.

- Endorsing another person's power can also be a source of power. A team lead delegating responsibilities to a junior associate endorses that associate, and may well achieve desired outcomes more effectively.

---

7. Folger et al., *Working Through Conflict*, 141.
8. Folger et al., *Working Through Conflict*, 143.
9. Folger et al., *Working Through Conflict*, 141.

Endorsement: Negotiating Power

- Much effort to influence can be met with a simple act of non-endorsement. Senator Talbert may use several tactics in a months-long effort to secure a fellow legislator's "yea" vote on an upcoming bill, only to see her vote "nay."
- Endorsement can create power that doesn't actually exist. If you convince me that your poker hand is better than mine, leading me to fold, I have fallen for your bluff.
- Empowerment is *more* of an act of endorsement of power than it is an act of power. Just like endorsement, delegation is an agreement that someone else has power. Endorsement, through delegation and empowerment, is necessary for expanding the power of the group.

These realities, and the fact that endorsement determines if someone else actually has power at all, contribute to the *irony of endorsement*: in many ways the endorsement of power can be more powerful than power itself.

QUI TACET CONSENTIRE VIDETUR: PASSIVE ENDORSEMENT

The Latin phrase *qui tacet consentire videtur*, as mentioned in chapter 4, roughly means "silence is consent." Colloquially, it means "that which I don't disagree with I agree with." At least two distinct challenges arise with passive endorsement:

- Passive endorsement is easily misinterpreted. A student listening to a professor in a lecture hall, for example, may be a sign that she understands what he is saying, or that she does not understand but is embarrassed to show it, or that she is disengaged and daydreaming. An introvert might be seen by others in a discussion as aloof, when he is actually deeply but passively engaged.
- Passive endorsement is very often easier than active negotiation of endorsement. Any egregious act of power, be it an unethical lapse in quality control, a sexist comment in the break

room, or clergy sexual assault on a child, often comes with a strong temptation to *turn a blind eye*. Silent non-response is often the easiest, safest, least consequential, most expedient option, on many levels, for all involved, especially those harmed.

THE VIOLENT CAVEAT WITHIN SOCIAL POWER

My social power is determined through the endorsement of those I seek to influence, with one troubling, ubiquitous caveat. "Excluding situations of unequal physical power and use of violence, power is a property of the social relationship rather than a quality of the individual."[10]

Violence is individual power employed as social power. It is individual power forced upon others, without their endorsement. Violence, be it a fist to the face, a knife to the leg, or a fire hose aimed at a crowd, is available to anyone willing to use it, including a four-year-old with a handgun. Violence argues that might makes right.

Someone may *resort to violence*, i.e., become violent as a last resort, such as when a thirteen-year-old Long Island girl fought off her adult male assailant. But very often violent power is just one of many options. In particular, when a party with legitimate power designated to them—e.g., a police officer, a football coach, the President of the United States—nevertheless resorts to violence, or threatens it or proposes others use it, that person earns many candid questions, including:

- "Did you indeed have no other choice?"
- "Do you not value the other sources of power designated to you?"
- "Do you simply like violence?"
- "What outcomes were you truly trying to achieve?"

---

10. Hocker and Wilmot, *Interpersonal Conflict*, 116.

Endorsement: Negotiating Power

Eric Hoffer is correct: "our sense of power is more vivid when we break a man's spirit than when we win his heart." Violence may be the most efficient means to this end. Violence is intrinsically coercive and competitive, especially on an identity level. Indeed, the visceral appeal of violent power is that it palpably and efficiently invalidates the victim by shoving aside any right to negotiate power. We have no uglier terms in our lexicon than those we use to describe violent power: rape, assault, murder, shaken baby syndrome, torture, incest, terrorism.

7
Regarding Other People's Power

> *When legitimately earned and properly used, rank is an important—often indispensable—organizational tool for accomplishing group goals. The more central rank is to achieving an organization's mission—for example, in the military—the more critical it is to distinguish it from rankism and to honor the former while eliminating the latter. Not every assertion of rank is rankist—only those that put the dignity of the high-ranking above those they serve.*
> —Robert Fuller, *All Rise: Somebodies, Nobodies, and the Politics of Dignity*

How I regard your power determines how I resist or endorse your efforts to "bring about desired outcomes," and how I marshal my sources of power in our relationship. Do I see your power competitively, as a threat to my own? Do I view your power through a consumeristic lens, believing that by giving you power I can expect you to take care of me and solve my problems? Do I regard your power comparatively, perhaps through a lens of rankism, believing that you merit less dignity than I do based on your status, gender, or skin color?

One party may instinctively regard another party's power from many orientations in the same relationship. Common ways I regard your power include:

Regarding Other People's Power

- comparative
- competitive
- collaborative
- designated
- consumeristic
- authoritarian
- referent
- insufficient
- expansive

These regards are merely descriptive lenses to assess how one party views another's power. They name general reasons why I am inclined to endorse or resist you power. These regards are not mutually exclusive. I can regard your power in more than one way, in the same relationship, at the same time, around different goals. Junior partners in the same law firm, for example, may collaborate tirelessly as a team for a client, while holding a keen comparative regard toward the other's status in the company. Congress and the president may debate and compete over immigration issues while collaborating on government funding, all while careful to address each other by their designated titles.

COMPARATIVE REGARD

A *comparative* or *sociometric regard* assesses my power by using others' power as a standard. It is heard in terms like blue collar, high end, and getting ahead.

A comparative regard can be objectively informative. Any adjective on a person's resume—*fast learner, seasoned, certified, expert*—reflects how she compares her power to others. Resumes themselves are vehicles to enable objective comparison, as are standardized tests. Formal hierarchy is stated in comparative terms—*middle management, entry level, C-suite*. When Robert

Fuller distinguishes between rank and rankism, he articulates how a comparative regard is simply necessary in organizational life.

The question Fuller asks is: Does lesser rank mean less dignity? A rankist, comparative regard is often implicit when stating informal status—*in-crowd*, *losers, coastal elites, illegals*. A comparative regard can combine with distrust to dehumanize and subhumanize others.

COMPETITIVE REGARD

A *competitive* or *distributive* regard believes that "power is fixed and finite and that there is only so much power to go around."[1] This zero-sum orientation, also called *power over*, *dominant*, and *either-or*, perceives that my power increases if I cause yours to decrease. My goal is to win against you.

A competitive regard is the intentional, aggressive, problem-solving manifestation of the comparative regard. Where a comparative regard assesses rank, a competitive regard seeks to establish rank. Who's the greatest? But this regard is commonplace: it drives sports, job searches, spelling bees, and almost any other setting involving valued scarce resources.

Hence this regard beckons me when I believe your power threatens my purposes and concerns. "The implicit assumption in this type of conceptualization of power is that power relations are inherently coercive and competitive; the more power A has, the less power available to B."[2]

This orientation is fascinating: stadiums are built to observe and participate in competition. This orientation is also highly motivating. Few forces push individuals and teams more than competing against another, even if the teams are made up of Girl Scouts selling cookies.

The person with a *competitive disposition*, or what Coleman calls a "chronic competitive (assertive) orientation to power,"[3]

1. Coleman, "Power and Conflict," 1st ed., 110.
2. Coleman, "Power and Conflict," 1st ed., 112.
3. Coleman, "Power and Conflict," 3rd ed., 152.

brings a win/lose perspective into any setting. If you are right then I must be wrong, and if I prove you wrong then I must be right. If I call you a loser then I must be a winner.

COLLABORATIVE REGARD

This regard, also called *power with*, *both-and*, and *mutual*, perceives that all parties' power can increase simultaneously. Or, at the least, your increasing power does not automatically mean mine decreases. Any successful team setting requires a collaborative regard. "Making the project work, moving toward mutual goals, and getting a new effort up and running require skills very different from those used with either/or power."[4] "With cooperation you actually create more power than the two of you could have created separately. Shared power is not a weak, tentative approach—it is powerful and energetic, and it requires great skill."[5]

Nevertheless, scholars describe that while a collaborating regard is the natural orientation in some cultures, and "often the first choice of women in our culture," a competitive regard is more common to men and to U.S. culture in general.[6]

DESIGNATED REGARD

We have a *designated regard* toward elected officials, the IRS, law enforcement, judges, and anyone else we formally give power to. I give authority to my employers, my county assessor, and my children's classroom teachers.

Designated power, or *given authority*, is the most:

- recognized form of power,
- recognized form of authority, and
- recognized way we regard power in others.

---

4. Hocker and Wilmot, *Interpersonal Conflict*, 9th ed., 109.
5. Hocker and Wilmot, *Interpersonal Conflict*, 9th ed., 109.
6. Hocker and Wilmot, *Interpersonal Conflict*, 9th ed., 110.

Section 2: Power in Context

This is as it must be. Given authority is often communicated loudly, for everyone to understand:

- a police officer's badge and distinctive uniform.
- a referee's striped shirt and whistle.
- a navy fleet admiral's distinctive 5-star insignia.

We need to know and agree who enforces the rules. Designated power is legitimate power formally, carefully given to another, for the benefit of the group. "When legitimately earned and properly used, rank is an important—often indispensable—organizational tool for accomplishing group goals."[7]

CONSUMERISTIC REGARD

> *Consumers give power away. They believe that their own needs can be best satisfied by the actions of others—whether those needs are elected officials, top management, social service providers, or the shopping mall. Consumers allow others to define their needs.*[8]

"A consumer is one who has surrendered to others the power to provide what is essential for a full and satisfied life."[9] "The essential promise of a consumer society is that satisfaction can be purchased. This promise runs so deep in us that we have come to take our identity from our capacity to purchase."[10]

As a consumer, I give power to you in exchange for your obligation to fulfill my wants and needs. Satisfaction guaranteed, or I get my money back. Many election campaign promises cater to a consumer mindset:

- "Once in office I'll take on the special interests and the lobbyists."

---

7. Fuller, *All Rise*, 10.
8. Block, *Community*, 63.
9. McKnight and Block, *Abundant Community*, 7.
10. McKnight and Block, *Abundant Community*, 9.

- "Elect me and I'll mend your roads and bridges."
- "The candidate for a brighter tomorrow."
- "Only I can fix it."

Consumers maintain power by taking it away from those who don't meet their expectations. Vote the bums out. Someone's head should roll. Demand the mayor resign.

AUTHORITARIAN REGARD

An *authoritarian regard* "involves an exaggerated need to submit to and identify with strong authority."[11] "Several traits characterize the syndrome: deference to authority, aggression toward outgroups, a rigidly hierarchical view of the world, and resistance to new experience."[12]

Viewed through the lens of Hofstede's power-distance cultures, those with an authoritarian regard appear to prefer a high power-distance settings: "Hierarchy in [such] an organization is seen as reflecting inherent inequalities, centralization is popular, subordinates expect to be told what to do and the ideal boss is a benevolent autocrat."[13]

Authoritarianism and Forty-Five

This regard appears to be a primary factor in Donald Trump's successful campaign as the forty-fifth President of the United States. Political researcher Matthew MacWilliams determined, "As early as 2016, researchers had identified 'the one weird trait that predicts whether you are a Trump supporter'—and it wasn't your gender, age, or religion. It was whether you had an authoritarian value set."[14] "And in a general election, Trump's strongman rhetoric will

11. Coleman, "Power and Conflict," 3rd ed., 145.
12. Pettigrew, "Social Psychological Perspectives on Trump Supporters," lines 89—91.
13. Hofstede Center, "Power Distance Dimensions."
14. Heimans and Timms, *New Power*, 170.

surely appeal to some of the 39 percent of independents in my poll who identify as authoritarians and the 17 percent of self-identified Democrats who are strong authoritarians."

> *While its causes are still debated, the political behavior of authoritarians is not. Authoritarians obey. They rally to and follow strong leaders. And they respond aggressively to outsiders, especially when they feel threatened. From pledging to "make America great again" by building a wall on the border to promising to close mosques and ban Muslims from visiting the United States, Trump is playing directly to authoritarian inclinations.*[15]

REFERENT REGARD

A *referent regard* forms from my admiration and strong identification with a person or group. I may reverence or even idolize someone, *place them on a pedestal*, or label myself a follower. I may want to behave, believe and perceive in ways they approve. The religious question *What would Jesus do?* demonstrates a referent regard. A ten-year-old girl displays a referent regard when choosing a role model, perhaps referring to him as her hero and saying, "Someday I am going to be like him." Efforts to mimic celebrities like John Wayne, Madonna, and Elvis Presley reflect a referent regard.

If I hold a strong referent regard for you, I give you immense power because I identify with you. I will "assume attitudes and beliefs" you hold, believe what you say, and dislike what you dislike.[16] I may need to deny or rationalize flaws in your character, because I have knitted my identity with yours. If someone else points your bad behaviors, I may angrily come to your defense. A person with referent regard "avoids discomfort and gains satisfaction by conformity based on identification"[17] with the person holding referent power.

15. MacWilliams, " One Weird Trait," lines 27–33.
16. French and Raven, "Bases of Social Power," 155.
17. French and Raven, "Bases of Social Power," 155.

INSUFFICIENT REGARD

The previous regards all focus on other people relationally: how I view my power in the context of yours. In contrast, an *insufficient regard* toward other people's power focuses on outcomes. In short, I assume you are incapable. I instinctively believe you are not able to achieve purposes I value. An insufficient regard is straightforward, underlying familiar terms:

- The *helicopter parent* who hovers over his child, practically completing her third-grade science fair project for her.
- The *lawnmower parent* who anticipates every challenge her child will face—e.g., sixth grade—and mows ahead of him to remove any obstacles.
- The *snoopervisor* manager who seems to lay in wait to spot what her employees are doing wrong.
- A guy *mansplaining* breastfeeding advice to a new mom.
- The *maternal gatekeeper* mom who assumes her husband cannot soothe their crying baby.
- The *ball hog* soccer player who would rather show off his footwork than pass to an open teammate.
- The *microaggression* of asking a black student on your college campus what sport they play.
- The *micromanager* who doesn't allow team members to address issues in any way but his.

I may assume you have insufficient power based on your height, gender, skin color, nationality, age, level of education, job title. "We endorse those we expect to be powerful and do not endorse those we expect to be weak."[18]

---

18. Folger et al., *Working Through Conflict*, 143.

SECTION 2: POWER IN CONTEXT

EXPANSIVE REGARD

An *expansive regard* defines success as another person gaining power. Teacher, coach, mentor: these roles model this regard.

The expansive regard seeks to make others "empowered and independent."[19] This is the dangerous orientation a flight instructor takes when she folds her arms as the plane descends toward the runway, forcing the student to land the plane. Expanding the power of a child is one of the primary responsibilities of a parent, knowing that someday those children will need to *make it on their own*. These examples illustrate the exponential potency of the expansive regard. With success, two people will know how to fly.

REDLINING: SELF-FULFILLING INSUFFICIENT REGARD

An insufficient regard, such as a boss micromanaging an employee, may be due to an instinctive, unconscious lack of trust in another party's power. However, my insufficient regard for your power can be deliberate, even aggressive. I may look for ways to make you feel insufficient, or of lower status compared to me. This may take place just between you and I, in the form of verbal abuse or *talking down to* or *belittling* you. An older male board member may listen to a new younger female board member make a proposal, and then call her a "feisty young thing" as a subtle means of invalidating her.

I may work with others in power, perhaps using our normative power and ecological power, to keep you and your kind *in your place* based on race or religion. The program of redlining demonstrates how an insufficient regard can be self-fulfilling and deliberate:

> In the 1930s, government surveyors graded neighborhoods in 239 cities, color-coding them green for "best," blue for "still desirable," yellow for "definitely declining" and red for "hazardous." The "redlined" areas were the ones local lenders discounted as credit risks, in large part because of the residents' racial and ethnic demographics. They also took

---

19. Coleman, "Power and Conflict," 1st ed., 110.

into account local amenities and home prices. Neighborhoods that were predominantly made up of African Americans, as well as Catholics, Jews and immigrants from Asia and southern Europe, were deemed undesirable.[20]

Susan Fiske and Robert Fuller articulate from different angles how an aggressive, competitive regard for others' power can inhabit a comparative, insufficient regard:

> *Stereotypes reinforce one group's or individual's power over another by limiting the options of the stereotyped group, so in this way stereotypes maintain power. People with power do not have to put up with them, but people without power are victims.*
>
> —Susan Fiske[21]

> *It becomes obvious that characteristics such as religion, color, gender, and age are merely excuses for discrimination, never its cause. Indeed, such features signify weaknesses only when there is a social consensus in place that handicaps those bearing them. Anti-Semitism, Jim Crow segregation, patriarchy, and homophobia are all complex social agreements that have functioned to disempower whole categories of people and keep them susceptible to abuse and exploitation.*
>
> —Robert Fuller[22]

HOW REGARDS DEFINE RELATIONSHIPS

How I regard your power impacts our relationship. Some subtle ways include:

- If I regard your power from a collaborative orientation, I may give you *the benefit of the doubt* when your actions are questionable. If I hold a referent regard for you, I may *look the other way* when you do something immoral or illegal.

20. Jan, "Redlining Was Banned 50 years Ago," lines 23–28
21. Fiske, "Controlling Other People," 623.
22. Fuller, *All Rise*, Introduction.

- Regards can easily be self-fulfilling. If I talk to you in an impatient, condescending way that reflects an insufficient regard, you may perceive yourself as insufficient. If I collaboratively assume you are worth listening to, you are more likely to believe you have something to say. If I show a competitive regard for your ability, you are only reasonable to adopt a competitive regard toward mine.

EXPANSIVE AND INSUFFICIENT REGARDS = EMPOWERMENT

At first glance, an insufficient regard toward another's power may seem contradictory or even the opposite of an expansive regard. But the two are symbiotic: the expansive regard exists because insufficiency exists. A youth baseball coach with an expansive regard expects, perhaps even enjoys, a bunch of kids who begin with little ability to play the game. A math teacher would be in a bad position if her students came in already knowing the material she plans to teach them. An expansive leader expects to escort those she leads from insufficient to sufficient power.

8

Dependence: Power's Revealing Mirror

> *[Harvey Weinstein] could make or break a star, he had huge personal capacity to green-light a project or sink it. He shaped the fortunes of an entire industry—and in turn that industry protected him even as he carried out a decades-long spree of alleged sexual harassment and assault.*
>
> —Jeremy Heimans and Henry Timms, *New Power*

Power is determined by context, and no concept illustrates this more than dependence. Power does not exist apart from some form of dependence. "Power is based on one person's dependence on resources or currencies that another person controls, or seems to possess."[1] My power in our relationship is a factor of your dependence on me. One party can change another's power by changing dependence, such as when country invests in solar energy research to *reduce dependence* on foreign oil. One party can also increase another party's power by increasing dependence, such as when a senior account executive entrusts a client to a junior executive he is mentoring.

---

1. Hocker and Wilmot, *Interpersonal Conflict*, 116.

In this way, dependence acts as a mirror to power, and this mirror can be uncomfortably revealing. For example, the high-power party in a group may well be the high-dependence party too. A shipping manager may have the most formal power in the shipping department, but also the most to lose if the department does not perform to certain standards. Hence this manager's true management style may be influenced more by her dependence than her authority.

Indeed, if power within a relationship is a distressing topic to discuss, it may well be because it implicitly addresses dependence within the same relationship. The anxious discomfort a job candidate experiences before and during an interview with the CEO is due to the dependence the candidate feels, as much or more than the relative power of the interviewer. When a young couple sits down to *define the relationship*, they are preparing to reveal, at least implicitly, how each does and does not want to depend on the other.

INVOLUNTARY DEPENDENCE

If my dependence on you is involuntary, I cannot remove myself from some aspect of our interdependent relationship. I must depend on you in some way, regardless of whether I trust you. I may even distrust you. You influence me, either directly or indirectly, in some way I cannot control. As such, I am forced to endorse your power.

Dictatorships, monopolies, prisons, and parenthood are examples of *involuntary dependence* settings. In these settings, certain survival needs—e.g., food, water, safety—can be met only by the high-power party.

Settings like these are often offset by some form of accountability, either formal or informal, and some sense of responsibility by the high-power party. Prisons are subject to federal oversight, for example. Other countries may impose sanctions on a violent dictator. Parents usually feel a deep, even sacrificial level of responsibility to their children.

But these examples imply the inherent dangers of involuntary dependence. Sans responsibility and effective accountability, settings defined by involuntary dependence are easily abused by the high-power party. Lord Acton warns that "absolute power tends to corrupt absolutely." This absolute power could not exist without absolute involuntary dependence.

TRUST BUILDING BEFORE INVOLUNTARY DEPENDENCE

Relationships commonly involve some aspect of involuntary dependence. Passengers on a plane in flight must depend on their pilot. A surgical patient is involuntarily dependent on the surgeon.

In these settings, considerable effort is put into instilling trust before involuntary dependence begins. A surgeon hones her *bedside manner* to calm a patient. Pilots wear crisp uniforms and hats that communicate capability and a military regimen. A candidate for office must establish trust in order to be elected to a position that will produce involuntary dependence among her constituents.

VIOLENCE AND INVOLUNTARY DEPENDENCE

Violence, or the threat of violence, is an attempt to establish involuntary dependence. This may be in some legitimate form, e.g., police forcing a dangerously drunk driver off the road, or in illegitimate form, e.g., a kidnapper tying up his victim.

Involuntary dependence inhabits most if not all settings involving abuse, be it emotional or physical. Involuntary dependence is implied in the key question often asked within abuse settings: How does the abused party escape?

- Does a bullied student move to another school, or stay inside at lunch?
- Does the sexually harassed coworker quit her job?
- Does a promising young starlet abandon her life-long ambitions as an actor, or engage in multiple unwanted sexual

encounters with a coercive producer until her career is established? Does this equal consent?

- Do citizens of a country flee their ancestral homes and become refugees to escape a violent dictator?
- Does the nine-year-old son listen to his drunk stepfather beat his mother, or does he shoot him, or does he run away and abandon her?

These questions help illustrate the magnitude of the dilemmas faced in circumstances of involuntary dependence. What must a person abandon to change their circumstances—school? job? home? community? ambitions? identity?

VOLUNTARY DEPENDENCE: A.K.A. TRUST

If my dependence is *voluntary*, I am choosing to depend on you. The more familiar terms for voluntary dependence are trust and faith. I place myself at risk, to some small or ultimate degree, by choosing to become dependent on your power. In this way, trust is perhaps the simplest yet most authentic form of endorsement.

I can choose to maintain trust, trust you more, trust you less, or *lose faith* altogether. All these changes re-define your power in our relationship. Conversely, your power, and my dependence on you, can increase as long as trust remains steady and voluntary. Lord Acton's fears about absolute power corrupting cannot be fully realized as long as dependence is voluntary, because your power is dependent on my faith in you.

Voluntary and involuntary dependence often coexist in significant relationships. As described before, a surgeon's bedside manner and the pilot's starched uniform are means to build trust prior to when the relationship enters that phase of involuntary dependence.

SOCCER PARENTS ON DEPENDENCE

The dependence you place in me in our relationship is likely different than the dependence I place in you, based on our differing

Dependence: Power's Revealing Mirror

goals, needs, concerns, etc. Understanding these differences in dependence does much to illuminate the true power dynamics in our relationship.

For example, a soccer player son may depend on his parents for equipment and transportation to practice and games, but the parents may depend on the son's performance for recognition from friends and other parents. If so, the son's dependence is outcome-based and the parents' dependence is identity-based.

Who needs whom more? Whose dependence is higher?

All the ways the parents support and motivate the son, for better or worse, are understood more fully by assessing the nature of their dependence, rather than by weighing their relative power. Their use of power—legitimate power to make him go to practice, informal coercive power when yelling at him to play better—may be factors of their high dependence on him for their esteem. Reciprocally, his level of play may have more to do with their approval or admonishment than with his own enjoyment of the game. These examples also illustrate the multifaceted connection between power and identity.

HARVEY WEINSTEIN ON DEPENDENCE

To understand the connection between endorsement, trust-based power, distrust-based power, and involuntary dependence in all of its complexity, it helps to return to Heimans and Timms's description of Harvey Weinstein's power:

> He could make or break a star, he had huge personal capacity to green-light a project or sink it. He shaped the fortunes of an entire industry.[2]

The power-dependence relationship Weinstein had with his victims was particularly nuanced. He had worked his way into a position where the whole film industry, not just the aspiring women within it, was involuntarily dependent on his power. Hence he could open any door for those he chose. This immense, beneficial,

---

2. Heimans and Timms, *New Power*, 2.

trust-based power had to be weighed, by his victims, against his coercive demands for sex.

Ordinarily, *distrust* and involuntary dependence go hand in hand. But in Weinstein's case, his victims were involuntarily dependent upon him because they *trusted* his power within the industry. Because they believed, rightly, that he had the ability to launch or ruin their careers, many young women were involuntary dependent on him.

DEPENDENCE IS DETERMINED BY THE DEPENDENT

Just like power in a relationship, dependence can fluctuate on a moment-to-moment basis. The dependence an airplane passenger places in an airline pilot is voluntary when a ticket is purchased. It increases when a passenger boards, and increases again when the airplane doors are closed. For many, dependence becomes involuntary at this point. Dependence increases as the plane pulls away from the terminal, jumps yet again the moment the wheels leave the ground, and may spike again as the plane approaches its landing.

Further, dependence may be sensed differently by different people. Factors like life experiences, gender, and age make experiencing dependence unique to the individual. A young woman, for example, may rightly be much more cautious about getting into a ride-share vehicle than an older man. Returning to the airplane example, one person may sense an anxiety spike when the doors are closed, another may sense this when the plane lifts off. A third may sleep through the whole thing even though her dependence fluctuates in precisely the same ways as the others.

Elections and Dependence

Dependence is voluntary to those who chose it, and involuntary to those who didn't. If, for example, the presidential candidate you voted for wins the election, you feel a sense of voluntary dependence toward that person while in office. If the presidential

Dependence: Power's Revealing Mirror

candidate I voted for lost, I feel involuntarily dependence, perhaps accompanied by some level of anxiety, toward the same president. If that president makes a questionable policy decision, you may be inclined to give the benefit of the doubt, where I raise the alarm.

Dependence, both involuntary and voluntary, can help make sense of the polarization this country feels during any particular presidency. It merits noting that any president, as the leader of the whole country, bears chief responsibility for reducing polarization, at least not increasing it, and certainly not leveraging it.

THE PRINCIPLE OF LEAST INTEREST: WALLER AND HILL

> *Your dependence on another person is a function of the importance of the goals the other can influence and the availability of other avenues for you to accomplish what you want.*[3]

Waller and Hill's *principle of least interest* states that the individual least invested in a personal relationship has the most power, and the person most invested must work harder to maintain it.[4] This principle, originally derived from studying informal relationships, sheds a revealing light on dependence in formal relationships as well.

The principle of least interest describes subtle but keenly felt challenges for those with legitimate power: leaders, executives, managers. These roles often have the highest formal power in a group, but they may well come with the highest dependence as well:

- The leader is dependent on those she leads. The group's formal goals likely matter more to the leader than to anyone else in the group.
- The leader may well be involuntarily dependent. The leader is responsible for the group's goals, and this group is her *only avenue* available to fulfill those obligations.

---

3. Hocker and Wilmot, *Interpersonal Conflict*, 9th ed., 116.
4. Heath, *Rational Choice and Social Exchange*, 24.

- Non-leaders may have very low dependence. The group's goals may matter less, even much less, to them. Employees may not get the measurable performance incentive packages that managers do. And if workers can easily find jobs elsewhere, they may hold significant power over the manager.

- If those being lead bring consumeristic and/or authoritarian regards to their view of the leader, they may sense no responsibility for the success or failure of the group, other than to retain or depose the formal leader.

SALARY AS DEPENDENCE

Money is power, the saying goes. But money should also be understood as a currency of dependence. In the movie *Office Space*, for example, the boss can serenely and repeatedly tell the main character on Friday at 4:58 p.m. to come in on Saturday morning, because he depends on a paycheck. When an employee uses her salary to pay her lease, finance a car payment, and buy food, she may reasonably regard herself as being in a state of high, even involuntary dependence on her company.

In some settings only the leader is salaried, and those led do so voluntarily. Examples of such settings are common: elected-electorate, pastor-congregation, and teacher-student-parent. The principle of least interest shines a particularly revealing light on these settings. In many practical ways, these leaders depend on the group more than those led.

Those with a consumeristic regard at once cripple and thrive in these settings. This is in part because the leaders' salaries in these settings are often paid, directly or indirectly, *by* those they are leading.

Such settings have the distinct potential to become skewed. The teacher may put more concern and effort into the student's academic achievement than the student does. The pastor may come to be seen as the only minister in the congregation. A mayor may be expected to resolve communal problems—end racism, stop gun violence—single-handedly.

9

Identity, Face, and Power

So Naaman [travelling from Syria to Israel, seeking a cure for his leprosy] went with his horses and chariots and stopped at the door of Elisha's house. Elisha sent a messenger to say to him, "Go, wash yourself seven times in the Jordan, and your flesh will be restored and you will be cleansed."

But Naaman went away angry and said, "I thought that he would surely come out to me and stand and call on the name of the Lord his God, wave his hand over the spot and cure me of my leprosy. Are not Abana and Pharpar, the rivers of Damascus, better than all the waters of Israel? Couldn't I wash in them and be cleansed?" So he turned and went off in a rage.

Naaman's servants went to him and said, "My father, if the prophet had told you to do some great thing, would you not have done it? How much more, then, when he tells you, 'Wash and be cleansed'!"

—2 Kings 5:9–13 (NIV)

Section 2: Power in Context

Peter T. Coleman defines power as "the ability to bring about desired outcomes."[1] And few outcomes could be more keenly desired than a miraculous cure for leprosy. All Naaman has to do is go and bathe in the River Jordan.

But Elisha offends him by showing no respect for his identity. He causes Naaman to lose face by not greeting him personally. And because of this, Naaman walks away *in a rage*, preferring in that moment to keep his leprosy.

In doing so, Naaman demonstrates one aspect of the connection between identity and power. Identity and face concerns can be more important than any other desired outcome. This core importance of identity and face can be heard in declarations like *death before dishonor* and Live Free or Die. This is just one of several reasons understanding identity and face concerns is crucial to a practical understanding of power.

FACETS OF IDENTITY

Bernard Bass said, "There are almost as many definitions of leadership as there are persons who have attempted to define the concept."[2] The same should be said for identity. Varied terms like *gender identity, identity politics, identity crisis,* and *identity theft* help illustrate this.

To understand and appreciate identity, it helps to break the concept of identity down into interwoven facets:

- personal, or psychological identity
- social identity
- shared identity
    - collective identity
    - institutional identity
- face concerns

---

1. Coleman, "Power and Conflict," 1st. ed., 112.
2. Bass, "Concepts of Leadership," 3.

- positive face
- negative face

Before proceeding it must be emphasized that these facets of identity overlap, often completely. When someone identifies herself a Lakota Sioux, for example, she is at once describing her personal, social, shared, collective, and institutional identity.

Personal or Psychological Identity

> *The measure of a man's real character is what he would do if he knew he would never be found out.*
> —Thomas Babington Macaulay

This facet of identity is heard in terms of self: self-concept, self-respect, self-assured, self-image, and self-aware. My personal identity is a life-long evolution of values, beliefs, lessons learned, character development, acceptance, learning, awareness of vices, etc. Henri-Frédéric Amiel was talking about personal identity when he said, "Dare to be what you are, and learn to resign with a good grace all that you are not and to believe in your own individuality." "Identity involves a sense of continuity, or the feeling that one is the same person today that one was yesterday or last year (despite physical or other changes)."[3]

Erik Erikson describes personal or psychological identity as beginning to form through the struggle of role confusion during adolescence.[4] The sometimes resistant ways teenagers relate to parents and peers has much to do with establishing psychological identity.

Social Identity

> *Image is everything.*
> —Andre Agassi

---

3. Vanderbos, "Identity," lines 3–5.
4. Ragelienė, "Links of Adolescents Identity."

Section 2: Power in Context

Terms like reputation, image, and stature reflect social identity. Do you respect me as intelligent, stylish, talented, wealthy? Am I accepted, appreciated, approved of? Do I belong here?

In this way social identity is to personal identity what social power is to individual power. My personal identity and individual power are my possessions. My social identity and social power are negotiated within relationship, and hence dependent upon others' endorsement.

Shared Identity

> *The greatest generation was formed first by the Great Depression. They shared everything—meals, jobs, clothing.*
> —Tom Brokaw

Who am I because of those I am connected to? Who shares my values, beliefs, worldview. gender, race, race-based fears, sexual preference, taste in music? Coloradoan is a shared-identity term, as are millennial and Yankees fan.

Shared identity is also concerned with how your actions and reputation reflect on me. Whom do I wish I was not associated with? We use disparaging terms for those who reflect negatively on us: *bad egg, black sheep* of the family, *stain* on the family name, *bad seed*.

Collective Identity

> *Nothing in life is more liberating than to fight for a cause larger than yourself, something that encompasses you but is not defined by your existence alone.*
> —John McCain

Collective identity is that aspect of shared identity that "derives from its members' common interests, experiences, and solidarities."[5] What causes do I and others feel strongly about, even if we never

---

5. Whooley, "Collective Identity," lines 1–3.

meet? What groups have I joined based on my beliefs and loyalties? Collective identity is heard in terms like deplorables and Bronco fans and *Semper Fidelis*. This is the facet of identity behind movements like Black Lives Matter and #MeToo, and the "new power" dynamics Heimans and Timms describe.

Institutional Identity

> *Ultimately, America's answer to the intolerant man is diversity, the very diversity which our heritage of religious freedom has inspired.*
> —Robert Kennedy

Where collective identity appears to be based more on values I consciously adopt, the institutional facet of my shared identity is based on groups established over generations and centuries: nationality, religion, tradition, heritage. What groups were both my great uncle and I born into?:

- "I'm a Sunni-Muslim."
- "I'm Asian-American."
- "I'm seventh-generation Kansan."

Returning to Erikson's concept of role confusion during adolescence, establishing my psychological or personal identity appears to involve wrestling with aspects of the collective and institutional aspects of my identity that I was born into:

- "I grew up Hindu but became a Christian in college."
- "My parents disowned me when I came out. But I'm still close with my sisters."
- "My parents, aunts, and uncles are all raving liberals, so Thanksgivings are tough anymore."

Section 2: Power in Context

FACE CONCERNS: IDENTITY IN THE MOMENT

Face concerns encompass my identity concerns as we interact in this moment. Is your tone of voice communicating respect, impatience, arrogance? Are you treating me like a child? Microaggressions are felt on the face level.

Within their oft-cited *Politeness Theory*, Brown and Levinson define face much like social identity, as "the public self-image every member wants to claim for himself."[6] Face concerns are heard in terms like approval, validation, recognition, respect, etc. The vital, immediate importance of face concerns can be felt in the bracing terms we use to describe face loss:

insulted	ashamed	offended	embarrassed
ignored	undermined	humiliated	invalidated
disgraced	slighted	wounded	demeaned
degraded	dehumanized	dishonored	taken for granted
denigrated	silenced	overlooked	rejected

Face loss, like that experienced by Naaman when Elisha declines to open his door to him, often:

- occurs in a moment,
- comes as a surprise,
- overwhelms all other desired outcomes within the interaction.

Naaman demonstrates the last point emphatically. Because he feels insulted, he refuses even to benefit from Elisha's remedy, though he never questions if that remedy will work.

Naaman's face loss is related to his institutional identity as much as any other aspect of his identity. He indicates this when he asks, "Are not Abana and Pharpar, the rivers of Damascus, better than the rivers of Israel?" Evidently Elisha has offended not just Namaan but all of Syria, just by not coming to the door. Whenever someone displays surprised, intense anger—or outright rage as in Naaman's case—a safe question to ask is: How has this person lost face?

6. Brown and Levinson, *Politeness*, 61.

Brown and Levinson argue that face is so important to each of us that we mutually, carefully steward one another's face concerns as we interact. "In general, people cooperate in maintaining face in interaction, such cooperation being based on mutual vulnerability of face."[7] You work hard to avoid embarrassing me, and I do the same with you. We say "please," "thank you," "you're welcome," and "excuse me," and we drill our kids to do so as well. All of these learned, face-saving gestures indicate the sensitive, delicate, constant nature of face concerns. Manners are about showing respect, and very much about stewarding another person's face concerns.

Negative and Positive Face

Brown and Levinson differentiate between *negative face* and *positive face*. My *positive face* concerns encompass my need for others to regard me favorably as we communicate, "crucially including the desire for that self-image to be appreciated and approved of."[8] Positive face covers a vast spectrum of conscious and unconscious concerns we have as we interact. Did you disrespect me? Did you make me feel inferior? Do you use a condescending tone of voice, or appear aloof? Face concerns often play out on the relational, paraverbal, and proxemic level.

Negative face concerns, in contrast, reflect my desire in the moment for "freedom of action and freedom from imposition."[9] When someone cuts in front of me in the check-out line, does not respect my personal space, or drives too slowly in the car ahead of me, my reaction is motivated by my negative face concerns. You are disrespecting me by how you are interfering with me. Declarations like *Don't tread on me* and *Live Free or Die*, the New Hampshire state motto, both cater to negative face concerns.

Returning to the example of Naaman, he demonstrates how positive and negative face concerns overlap in the same interaction. His rage is about positive face loss because Elisha did not come to

---

7. Brown and Levinson, *Politeness*, 61.
8. Brown and Levinson, *Politeness*, 61.
9. Brown and Levinson, *Politeness*, 61.

see him. But Naaman's face loss is also about negative face. He is upset at the imposition of having to go away and bathe: "I thought that he would . . . wave his hand over the spot and cure me of my leprosy."

HOW POWER MATTERS TO IDENTITY AND FACE

The connection between power and identity is heard in empowering verbs like encourage, strengthen, invigorate and inspire. This connection is also heard in belittling verbs like humiliate, demean, invalidate, undermine, disrespect and bully. To bully is to treat identity as a scarce resource; I elevate mine by attacking yours.

Power and identity converge in numerous other deep, even existential ways:

- My identity goals drive my needs and wants for power. My ambitions, ideals, interests, aspirations and values all contribute to my identity. These also fuel my desire to gain specific forms of social power and individual power.

- My social identity concerns make me dependent on others. I negotiate my reputation with others, but they make the final decision. Whether I am esteemed, feared, or trusted is ultimately not my question to answer. My social identity is subject to those I respect, and to those I disrespect. And in this hyperconnected world, my social identity can be impacted by people I don't even know.

- My personal identity moderates my dependence on others. My inner sense of worth, my self-respect, my self-image are factors of my personal identity. As will be argued later in this chapter, the stronger these are, the more my personal identity forms a grounded foundation for my social identity. The less solid my psychological identity is, the more my identity as a whole is dependent upon others.

- The strong emotions that drive conflict are often identity related, as Naaman exemplifies. Identity concerns are why we can't talk politics or religion at Thanksgiving. Whenever some form of intense anger—rage, fury, lashing out—is expressed in conflict, good questions to ask are: How was this person's identity harmed? How has this person lost face? Face loss can prompt an intense, even violent competitive regard, seen in the desire to *get even, get revenge, make them pay*. Professional athletes are known to compete harder against teams that insulted them by passing over them in the draft.

- Identity and face goals are our most valued concerns. When someone declares "death before dishonor," she is saying even her life is less important than her identity. To "sell your soul" is to sacrifice your character and reputation for some lesser desired outcome, like riches or fame. If one person causes another to lose face, it can sever family relationships, end friendships, and derail transactions.

- My identity suffers when I perceive I have low power. "Without some exercise of power in your interpersonal relationships, you would soon feel worthless as a person."[10] Feeling ignored, invisible, invalid, taken for granted, i.e., low power, has a caustic effect on my identity.

- Resistance to power is often fueled, at least in part, by face and identity concerns. "Resistance is often used to forge or sustain valued conceptions of self in the face of situational pressures to do otherwise."[11] Rosa Parks's quiet, stubborn resistance was fueled by identity concerns.

- Expansive power settings, e.g., the classroom, the mentoring program, on the job training sessions, change my identity in the process of making me more capable. Settings that exist to expand my power, be it through education, training, discipleship, mentoring, etc., exist to change my identity. We use familiar terms—*transformational leadership*, *learning organization*, *growth mindset*—to name the connection between expansive power settings and identity change.

10. Hocker and Wilmot, *Interpersonal Conflict*, 116.
11. Ashforth and Mael, "Power of Resistance," 92.

Section 2: Power in Context

01/06/2021: WHEN FACETS OF IDENTITY FIGHT

As described in Chapter 1, power is the "architecture" of conflict. And identity concerns are very often at the root of conflict. Any country's defense spending is to protect and establish its institutional identity.

However, conflict fueled by different facets of identity also merits close study. We use terms like polarization, tribalism, identity politics, and sectarian violence to describe when those with competing collective identities share the same institutional identity. The deadliest, most-defining conflict the United States ever experienced was its own Civil War. Ireland's history is defined by the Troubles. Rwanda will long be synonymous with genocide. On January 6, 2021, United States citizens who shared a certain collective identity violently attacked the United States' institutional identity.

Conflict between those with the same shared identity, e.g., family, but differing personal identities, e.g., republican, Pentecostal, can also become shrill and entrenched. This level of inter-identity conflict is why we can't talk politics and religion at Thanksgiving dinner.

Understanding conflict involving different facets of identity helps reveal the differing reasons we seek power, and the differing forms of power we seek. And the most core-level, existential conflict, the competition that may define all the others, is between each person's own psychological (personal) identity and their social identity. Six voices speak next on why personal identity should be the first concern.

JOHN WOODEN ON PERSONAL IDENTITY

> *Be more concerned about your character than your reputation, because your character is who you really are, while your reputation is merely what others think you are.*
> —John Wooden

John Wooden, along with David Brooks, Maya Angelou, a candid young Coloradoan named Amelia, Abraham Maslow, and Murray

Bowen speak to how social identity and personal identity will always compete, but how we are better off if the latter wins.

John Wooden's admonishment to be more concerned about character than reputation encapsulates how personal identity must be foundational in forming my overall identity. My social identity is determined in negotiation with others, making me in that way dependent on them. Others decide my reputation.

In contrast, my personal identity, my strength of character, my mettle, is determined by me alone, through my own individual power. The social power others have over me depends upon the degree to which I value my personal identity over my social identity.

We have choice words for those whose social identity does not match their personal identity: hypocrite, fake, two-faced, poser, con artist, cheat, *wolf in sheep's clothing,* phony. We also have unflattering terms—shallow, gilded, cosmetic, superficial—for those who place higher or sole value on their social identity. In contrast, we use terms like integrity, principled, guileless, and straightforward to describe those whose social identity stands in the shadow of their personal identity.

DAVID BROOKS ON PERSONAL IDENTITY

The tension between personal and social identity is also heard in David Brooks's delineation between the "resume virtues" and the "eulogy virtues" in his book *The Road to Character*:

> *The resume virtues are the ones you list on your resume, the skills that you bring into the job market and that contribute to external success. The eulogy virtues are deeper. They're the virtues that get talked about at your funeral— whether you are kind, brave, honest and faithful; what kind of relationships you formed.*[12]

Brooks goes on to make a more pointed distinction between the person defined by personal identity and the person driven by social identity needs, in differentiating between self-effacement and self-promotion.

12. Brooks, *Road to Character*, Introduction.

SECTION 2: POWER IN CONTEXT

> *The self-effacing person is soothing and gracious, while the self-promoting person is fragile and jarring. Humility is freedom from the need to prove you are superior all the time, but egotism is a ravenous hunger in a small space— self-concerned, competitive, and distinction-hungry. Humility is infused with lovely emotions like admiration, companionship, and gratitude.*[13]

How does humility affect my need for social power? What freedom comes with the ability to laugh at myself, to not take myself too seriously, to comfortably use my own mistakes as tools to teach others? How much lighter does the whole world become when I begin to take my self lightly?

MAYA ANGELOU AND AMELIA ON PERSONAL IDENTITY

Beyond David Brooks and John Wooden, a third argument for a foundation of personal identity is presented through a 1973 interview between journalist Bill Moyers and author Maya Angelou.

> Bill Moyers: *Do you belong anywhere?*
> Maya Angelou: *I haven't yet.*
> Bill Moyers: *Do you belong to anyone?*
> May Angelou: *More and more . . . I belong to myself. I'm very proud of that. I am very concerned about how I look at Maya. I like Maya very much.*[14]

The self-defining struggle between personal and social identity is heard in Angelou's careful response to Moyer's questions. Is who I am based on belonging, on others' acceptance and approval, or my own approval of myself? How do I feel about myself, really? Do I like myself? What matters more to me: my image or my self-image?

Contrasting Angelou's assessment that she belongs to herself, consider the effort and focus described by a candid, vulnerable young woman named Amelia in a Colorado Public Radio interview on the topic of teen stress:

13. Brooks, *Road to Character*, 8.
14. Angelou and Moyers, "Conversation with Maya Angelou."

IDENTITY, FACE, AND POWER

I will actually take pictures so I can post them on my Snapchat and people can swipe up and then I can feel better about myself.[15]

Maya Angelou's words—"I belong to myself"—describe an overall identity founded upon personal identity. The teenager above describes an identity founded upon social identity. How she regards herself is dependent upon how others regard her.

This candid teenager, possibly experiencing the depth of Erikson's role confusion, provides a stark, succinct illustration of how social identity needs create dependence. She has given others the power to determine how she feels about herself. Further, she illustrates how social media facilitates and promotes this dependence.

Returning to Maya Angelou, her words imply that my personal identity is not something I just control or decide, but instead something I negotiate within myself over my lifetime.

ABRAHAM MASLOW ON PERSONAL IDENTITY

To explore this wrestling between psychological and social identity from a fourth angle, it helps to return to Maslow's hierarchy of needs. Maslow categorizes human needs in five levels, with the most basic needs at the bottom, and the most difficult to attain at the top (as listed below):

- Level 5—Self-actualization needs: self-fulfillment, self-awareness, creativity
- Level 4—Esteem needs: accomplishment, recognition
- Level 3—Belonging needs: friends, relationships, intimacy
- Level 2—Safety needs: security, shelter from harm
- Level 1—Physiological needs: food, water, warmth, rest

While this hierarchy has been debated since its inception, one general pattern related to social and personal identity merits mention here:

---

15. Brundin, "Colorado Teens," lines 35–36.

- Physiological and Safety needs, the bottom two levels, can be met through individual power means if necessary.
- Belonging needs (third level) all correspond with social identity and social power. These needs, e.g., friendship and intimacy, are all met through relationship.
- Esteem needs (fourth level) portray an evenly split mix of social identity needs and personal identity needs. "According to Maslow, esteem needs include two components. The first involves feeling self-confidence and feeling good about oneself. The second component involves feeling valued by others; that is, feeling that our achievements and contributions have been recognized by other people."[16] In terms of power and dependence, the needs that make up this Esteem level are a 50/50 blend of personal identity needs (e.g., self-confidence) met through individual power, and social identity needs (e.g., recognition, intimacy) that depend on relationships.
- Self-actualization, the highest level, is solely about personal identity and individual power. It is defined by needs—e.g., self-fulfillment, self-awareness, creativity—met independently from others.

This begs a defining question. Can that person whose overall identity is founded primarily upon social identity, for whom "image is everything," ever meet the needs that define self-actualization? Can Maslow's summit ever be reached by the person who values social identity more foundationally than personal identity?

MURRAY BOWEN ON PERSONAL IDENTITY

The Bowen theory concept *differentiation of self* offers a fifth angle from which to appreciate the tension between psychological identity and social identity, along with the foundational importance of the former. Bowen's conclusions also do much to illustrate the connection between identity, dependence, and power.

16. Hopper, "Maslow's Hierarchy of Needs Explained."

Identity, Face, and Power

Family systems theory pioneer Murray Bowen defined the concept of self-differentiation as "the degree to which one is able to balance (a) emotional and intellectual functioning and (b) intimacy and autonomy in relationships."[17] "On an interpersonal level, differentiation of self refers to the ability to experience intimacy with and independence from others."[18]

To grasp this concept, it helps to compare descriptions of people at different levels of self-differentiation:

- "The individuality of very well differentiated people is developed to the point that they can be responsible for themselves and not fault others for their own discontents. Togetherness needs are such that, while people are attracted to and interested in one another, their functioning is not dependent on each other's approval."[19]

- "As differentiation decreases, individuality is less well developed, togetherness needs are stronger, emotional reactivity is more intense and more easily triggered, and subjectively based attitudes are more influential."[20]

- "The individuality of a very poorly differentiated person is practically non-existent. His emotional reactions are easily triggered, intense, and prolonged, and he has almost no psychological development that permits him to be a separate person. The togetherness needs of a very poorly differentiated person, which are overriding in their influence, are felt as deep yearnings to be loved, accepted and guided through life."[21] "A very poorly differentiated person has no capacity for autonomous functioning."[22]

- "At the very highest levels of differentiation, no matter what the intensity of emotional, feeling, and subjectively determined

---

17. Skowron and Friedlander, "Differentiation of Self Inventory," 235.
18. Skowron and Friedlander, "Differentiation of Self Inventory," 235.
19. Kerr and Bowen, *Family Evaluation*, 74–75.
20. Kerr and Bowen, *Family Evaluation*, 75.
21. Kerr and Bowen, *Family Evaluation*, 69.
22. Kerr and Bowen, *Family Evaluation*, 70.

SECTION 2: POWER IN CONTEXT

pressure from others to operate in other than a self-determined direction, the person can retain his autonomy."[23]

Though Bowen's concept of self-differentiation is not a direct reflection of the tension between personal and social identity, the similarity is informative. The well-differentiated person is more founded upon personal identity, less emotionally dependent on the assessment of others, and less easily triggered by the practical jostling that comes with social interaction. In short, such a person is less easily offended, insulted, demeaned, etc. The well-differentiated person is not impervious to the influence of others, but rather is able to weigh approval and disapproval from a more autonomous, rational foundation. In terms of identity and dependence, the overall identity of a poorly differentiated person appears to be founded more upon their social identity, and dependent on the approval / disapproval of others.

DON'T TREAD ON ME: NEGATIVE FACE VERSUS POWER

Negative face concerns, by their very definition, appear to resist power. Compare Brown and Levinson's definition of negative face with two definitions of power:

> *Power is the ability to change the behavior of others.*
> —Robert Vecchio[24]

> *Negative face is the want of every person that his actions be unimpeded by others. Also, "freedom of action and freedom from imposition."*
> —Brown and Levinson[25]

23. Kerr and Bowen, *Family Evaluation*, 70.
24. Vecchio, *Leadership*, 69.
25. Brown and Levinson, *Politeness*, 63.

Identity, Face, and Power

> *Individuals have power when they have access to resources that can be used to persuade or convince others, to change their course of action, or to prevent others from moving toward their goals in conflict situations.*
>
> —Folger, Poole and Stutman[26]

Note how the description of negative face pulls hard in the opposite direction against these definitions of power. Negative face concerns encompass that instinctive resistance one party has to another's attempts to influence them. This natural tension lends credence to the studied contention that workplace resistance is often a means to protect or enhance identity.[27]

While it could be said that negative face concerns oppose power, this understanding seems unnecessarily contentious. Indeed, many settings, especially formal leadership settings, come with the expectation of being imposed upon. An army private expects to take orders and carry them out. A waiter expects to wait tables. "Some task goals (e.g., getting people out of a burning building) are so dominant that face concerns may drop by the wayside. In some cases joining a group means accepting someone's authority (e.g., joining the army) regardless of face concerns."[28]

FACE GAIN

While we can lose face, Brown and Levinson point out that face can also be "enhanced"[29] as we interact. One person can bring about *face gain* by complimenting another, or validating by merely listening to her carefully. Many simple means can be used to instill in another person a favorable self-image in the moment.

Returning to the story of Naaman, his servants demonstrated a clever awareness of his face concerns in how they steered him back toward Elisha's prescription for his leprosy: "My father, if the prophet had told you to do some great thing, would you not have

---

26. Folger et al., *Working Through Conflict*, 140.
27. Ashforth and Mael, "Power of Resistance," 97–98.
28. Brown, email interview response, October 2013.
29. Brown and Levinson, *Politeness*, 61.

done it?" They point out that if Elisha had given Naaman a challenge that involved face gain, he would have done it without taking offense.

POWER IMBALANCE AND FACE

Face threat is the vulnerability I feel when I somehow place my identity at risk as we interact. Face threat names that terrified sensation one young person feels when asking someone to a school dance.

Face threat increases as power imbalance increases. For example, if you and I are staff accountants and share the same cubicle office space, asking you to loan me $20 for lunch may be easy enough. But if you are my regional vice president, asking to borrow $20 comes with much more face threat. "The greatest potential face threat is found when there is great social distance between the parties, the listener has more power than the speaker, and there is a great degree of imposition placed on the communicative request or act."[30]

If the power imbalance increases face threat, it can also increase *face gain*. One colleague saying "great idea" to another in a meeting brings some level of face gain, but the CEO saying the same thing means much more.

For a vivid example of power imbalance resulting in face gain, we can return to the beginning of chapter 5, and the story of President Obama bending down to allow five-year-old Jacob Philadelphia to touch his head. If both parties were five-year-old boys, this interaction would have been different. But this is the President of the United States. For his part, Jacob was so nervous that he found it difficult to speak. But the face gain he derived from the interaction was national celebrity.

IDENTITY AND MANIPULATION

Identity needs can be a source of coercive power for others. What value do you place on my approval, and how can I use this to coerce

---

30. Folger et al., *Working Through Conflict*, 175.

your behavior? Consider the coercive power of these identity-related questions:

- "Are you smart enough to figure this out?"
- "You're not chicken, are you?"
- "Are you man enough?"
- "Do you have what it takes?"

Each of these questions is my bid to gain power by placing your identity in question. Each of these questions uses your identity coercively against you. Consider four more deeply coercive questions:

- "Do you expect me to settle for this?"
- "Was it a mistake to depend on you?"
- "Don't you care that my sister has left me to do all the work?"
- "Did I raise you to treat me this way?"

These are double-bind, doubly coercive questions, because they declare that harm has already been done. Any response to these questions as asked must agree that you have *already* offended me.

If you are a polite person and these questions are directed at you, you may instinctively feel shame and high obligation to make amends. That is the coercive power in questions like these.

In describing the coercive use of face and identity, however, relational factors must be reiterated. Context must always be considered. In a relationship denoted by high trust, respect, and camaraderie, for example, questions like "Is that the best you've got?" and "Do you need me to bail you out again?" may be profound, ironic forms of encouragement.

IDENTITY AND RESISTANCE

When Rosa Parks refused to move from her seat to make way for a white person, her act of resistance was motivated by all facets of her identity—personal, social, shared, collective, and institutional. Further, she silently, resolutely acted on her valid negative face concerns: a desire for autonomy and freedom from imposition.

"Resistance is often used to forge or sustain valued conceptions of self in the face of situational pressures to do otherwise. At one extreme, resistance may be used to defend a relatively complete social identity . . . At the other extreme, resistance may be used to defend idiosyncratic aspects of one's psychological identity."[31] In short, resistance to power is often motivated by the need to establish or defend one's identity.

IS SHE COACHABLE?: RESISTANCE TO EMPOWERMENT

While identity and face dynamics impact any setting, they define expansive power settings most tangibly. The classroom, the flight simulator, the soccer practice field, and any other setting where a leader facilitates learning, exists to increase power. And that expanding power changes identity. When I earn my pilot's license or my high school diploma, I officially become more powerful. My accomplishments enhance my identity. I put on my cap and gown, or pin on my wings, so others will see me as more than I was. I now share identity with others who have accomplished this.

Then why do I resist growth? Why does a student skip math class? Why does a teenager roll his eyes when dad wants to show him how to change a tire? Why does a soccer player resent her coach when he pulls her aside to demonstrate better technique? Consider four reasons:

1. Resistance bolsters my existing identity. "Resistance is often used to forge or sustain valued conceptions of self in the face of situational pressures to do otherwise."[32] A *class clown* student may gain more in the moment by resisting the teacher's efforts than by learning.

---

31. Ashforth and Mael, "Power of Resistance," 92.
32. Ashforth and Mael, "Power of Resistance," 92.

2. My positive face concerns, my desire to be admired and approved of, don't like the vulnerability that accompanies learning. I don't want to look like I don't know something.
3. My negative face concerns instinctively resist instruction. I may just not like being told what to do or how to do it.
4. If I gain power, I gain vulnerability, in the form of increased expectations and responsibilities. If I have a pilot's license, someone is going to expect me to actually fly a plane. If I get my high school diploma, I am going to be asked about college or trade school plans. Increased expectations place all facets of my identity—personal, social, and shared—at increased risk.

Nevertheless, anyone entering any learning environment must understand that they are here not just to learn but to change their identity. He is here precisely to be imposed upon and improved upon. She is here to be more afterwards than she was before.

Expansive leadership settings exist to increase the power of those led, and increased power is itself a form of identity change. But each person's existing identity and negative face concerns can hinder or even derail this process. Is he coachable? Is she teachable? Can they take advice? These questions, though they outwardly address task goals and relationship goals, are actually questions of identity and face.

"CULTURE EATS STRATEGY FOR BREAKFAST": IDENTITY AND NORMATIVE POWER

Normative power, introduced in chapter 2, is a group's power over individuals who want to belong within it, i.e., people who want to share that group's identity. Peter Drucker's statement that "Culture eats strategy for breakfast"[33] reflects how normative power and collective identity do more to define a group than formally established outcome goals, even within a formal task-focused group like a business. Ashforth and Mael reflect Drucker's statement. They capture

---

33. Braun, "It's the Culture, Stupid," line 5.

Section 2: Power in Context

the potency of normative power and shared identity within an organization, in part by framing them in terms of coercive potential:

> What makes normative control so insidious is that, when complete, it is experienced not as externally imposed but as internalized and freely chosen . . . It insinuates itself into one's workplace identity such that to resist it is to be at war with oneself . . . It is this fusion of self and organization that makes normative control so appealing to organizations.[34]

Normative power, be it in the form of corporate culture, peer pressure or societal traditions, can be intensely and internally coercive. To be *at war with oneself* is to allow one's collective identity to attack one's personal identity.

Still, normative power, like any form of power, "is neither positive nor negative—power just is."[35] Normative power is the result of norms, and norms can be collaborative and redeeming. It is normative power that prompts an adult who catches a baseball hit into the stands to give the ball to a nearby child instead of keeping it. Normative power prompts soccer players on both sides to kneel while an injured player is down. Normative power indwells the Zulu communal kindness principle of *ubuntu*:

> In fact, the word ubuntu is just part of the Zulu phrase "Umuntu ngumuntu ngabantu," which literally means that a person is a person through other people. Ubuntu has its roots in humanist African philosophy, where the idea of community is one of the building blocks of society. Ubuntu is that nebulous concept of common humanity, oneness: humanity, you and me both.[36]

---

34. Ashforth and Mael, "Power of Resistance," 93.
35. Hocker and Wilmot, *Interpersonal Conflict*, 73.
36. Ifejika, "What Does Ubuntu Really Mean," lines 9–12.

10

Trust, Distrust, and Power

> *Kate knew how the girls felt about her. They were desperately afraid of her. She kept them that way. It was probable that they hated her, and that didn't matter either. But they trusted her, and that did matter. If they followed the rules she laid down, followed them exactly, Kate would take care of them and protect them. There was no love involved and no respect.*
>
> —John Steinbeck, *East of Eden*

Kate Trask, antagonist and "malformed soul" in John Steinbeck's novel, ponders how the women in her brothel at once trust her and highly distrust her. As she does, she illustrates the immense power she has over them as a result.

Kate's calculations, however heartless, demonstrate important truths about trust in relationships, including how:

- trust and distrust coexist in relationships,
- trust and distrust can both be extremely high within the same relationship,
- trust and distrust combine to form complex, tangled power dynamics.

Section 2: Power in Context

Most relationships are a fluid blend of trust and distrust, each fluctuating as the relationship evolves. And the blend of trust and distrust you feel toward me is probably not the same blend I feel toward you.

CBT, IBT, CBD, AND IBD: LEWICKI AND TOMLINSON

Lewicki and Tomlinson differentiate both trust and distrust into two forms, *calculus based* and *identification based*. These combine to form four types:

- calculus-based trust (CBT)
- calculus-based distrust (CBD)
- identification-based trust (IBT)
- identification-based distrust (IBD)

Calculus-based trust (CBT) is "a confident positive expectation regarding another's conduct. It is grounded in impersonal transactions, and the overall anticipated benefits of the relationship to be derived from the relationship are assumed to outweigh any anticipated costs."[1] This is the trust placed in a pharmacy to fill a prescription, or the oncoming driver to stay in their lane. CBT is the rational, reason-based trust placed in another party to perform as expected because it is in their best interests. CBT is called calculus-based because the party being trusted calculates the harm of betraying that trust. It is calculus-based reasoning to believe the particular airplane I'm boarding is safe because this airline would not be in business if they weren't very careful. Many companies depend on the CBT of their customers.

Identification-based trust (IBT) is "grounded in perceived compatibility of values, common goals, and positive emotional attachment to each other."[2] IBT is not rational, impersonal, and calculated like CBT. It is instead based on positive *emotional* attachment,

---

1. Lewicki and Tomlinson, "Trust, Trust Development, and Trust Repair," 112.
2. Lewicki and Tomlinson, "Trust, Trust Development, and Trust Repair," 112.

identification, and shared values. I place this trust in you because I believe you understand and empathize with me; my identity is safe with you. "Increased identification enables us to think like each other, feel like each other, and respond like each other."[3] "This form of trust can develop in working relationships if the parties know each other well, but it is most likely to occur in intimate, personal relationships."[4] This is the trust I place in those who either share my identity, or convince me they respect it.

Moving to distrust, *calculus-based distrust* (CBD) involves "a confident negative expectation regarding another's conduct. It is also grounded in impersonal transactions, and the overall anticipated costs to be derived from the relationship are assumed to outweigh the anticipated benefits."[5] This is the distrust I experience toward the driver who does not appear to be slowing down for me as I enter the crosswalk. If I tend to drive over the speed limit, this is the impersonal, transactional distrust I feel toward the patrolman up ahead.

Identification-based distrust (IBD) is "a confident negative expectation regarding another's conduct, grounded in perceived incompatibility of values, dissimilar goals, and negative emotional attachment to the other."[6] To some high or low degree, I feel unsafe around you because I don't identify with you. I sense that our beliefs or opinions or political leanings conflict. My identity is somehow threatened by you.

TRUST-BASED VERSUS DISTRUST-BASED POWER

Some forms of power require trust in the relationship. Examples of *trust-based power* include expertise, special skills, referent, and reward power. If you don't trust my skill as an auto mechanic, you won't allow me to dismantle your car's engine.

---

3. Lewicki and Tomlinson, "Trust, Trust Development, and Trust Repair," 109.
4. Lewicki and Tomlinson, "Trust, Trust Development, and Trust Repair," 112.
5. Lewicki and Tomlinson, "Trust, Trust Development, and Trust Repair," 112.
6. Lewicki and Tomlinson, "Trust, Trust Development, and Trust Repair," 112.

Distrust-based power, or coercive power, is based on *confident negative expectations*. How can I make your life unpleasant if you don't do what I want? How can I withhold valued rewards? How can I dispense punishments, formal or informal, physical or emotional?

Referent Power and IBT

Of all trust-based forms of power, referent power appears most closely associated with IBT specifically. Referent power "has as its basis the identification" of one person to another, and "by identification, we mean a feeling of oneness."[7] These descriptions of referent power by Raven and French closely correspond with Lewicki and Tomlinson's definition of identification-based trust, which is "grounded in perceived compatibility of values, common goals, and positive emotional attachment to each other."[8] Hence, IBT may well be at the heart of the emotional confidence I ascribe to someone I grant referent power to: an esteemed boss, a role model, a charismatic celebrity or political leader.

TRUST AND DISTRUST: HIGH AND LOW

Lewicki and Tomlinson describe how CBT, IBT, CBD, and IBD coexist in most ongoing relationships. Further, a relationship can be defined by high or low levels of each. For example, they describe a relationship with low CBT, low CBD, low IBT, and low IBD as "an arm's length relationship." In contrast, a relationship with low CBT, high CBD, high IBT, and low IBD is one they summarize as, "I love you but you're erratic and unpredictable."[9] The four coexisting types of trust, coupled with how any of them can be high or low, illustrate the complexity of any relationship.[10] Further, effectiveness of any form of trust-based and distrust-based power fluctuate according to these high and low levels.

7. French and Raven, "Bases of Social Power," 154.
8. Lewicki and Tomlinson, "Trust, Trust Development, and Trust Repair," 112.
9. Lewicki and Tomlinson, "Trust, Trust Development, and Trust Repair," 114.
10. Lewicki and Tomlinson, "Trust, Trust Development, and Trust Repair," 114.

Returning to the example provided by Steinbeck, Kate Trask and the girls in her brothel illustrated two of these variations, and the power dynamics that result. The girls' relationship with Kate could be described as:

- *High CBT*—Kate would take care of them and protect them, if they just kept up their end of the bargain.
- *High CBD*—They followed the rules she laid down, exactly, because they were desperately afraid of her.
- *Low IBT*—They likely knew they didn't matter to her. There was no love involved and no respect.
- *High IBD*—They were desperately afraid of her, and she kept them that way. It was probable that they hated her.

Lewicki and Tomlinson would classify this as a "dominant high distrust relationship" toward Kate. "Very distrusting, but bounded trusting transactions are possible."[11] To maintain what little power they had in the relationship, Kate's girls knew they had one narrow means: follow the rules exactly. Give her what she wanted. The ways Kate's girls felt toward her illustrate just how high distrust can be in a working relationship, so long as some level of CBT exists.

Meanwhile, Kate's relationship toward her girls would be:

- *High CBT*—She trusted them to perform their work as expected.
- *Low CBD*—She knew they would follow her rules.
- *Low IBT*—Kate had zero emotional attachment to them. That they were afraid of her did not matter. Nor did it matter if they hated her. No love and no respect.
- *Low IBD*—The girls pose no threat to Kate's identity. Their opinion of her does not matter to her.

Lewicki and Tomlinson label this combination of trust and distrust a "good working relationship,"[12] and Kate would likely have

---

11. Lewicki and Tomlinson, "Trust, Trust Development, and Trust Repair," 114.
12. Lewicki and Tomlinson, "Trust, Trust Development, and Trust Repair," 114.

agreed. She obtained every desired outcome she wanted and nothing she didn't from this arrangement. Kate and her girls demonstrate just how low IBT and IBD can be in a workable relationship. These trust and distrust lenses clarify in detail how each party views the relationship, and how different parties can view the same relationship very differently.

Kate further demonstrates how much power a person can have over others through a combination of high trust and high distrust.

IBD, IBT, AND FACETS OF IDENTITY

Lewicki and Tomlinson note that relationships are a complex mixture of these forms of trust and distrust, and that any instance of trust or distrust should be considered within the context of the larger specific relationship. They also stress that their theory of trust is still in relative infancy[13] and will benefit from further scrutiny. These cautions acknowledged, IBT and IBT merit closer examination.

HIGH IBT: THE POWER OF COLLECTIVE IDENTITY

Lewicki and Tomlinson's definition and description of high IBT in relationships sheds light on the power of *shared identity*, and more specifically *collective identity*. They characterize a relationship defined by high IBT in terms of loyalty, burden sharing, and "acting for each other,"[14] and use the vivid example of a person responding to a friend's loss of face: "A true affirmation of the strength of [IBT] between parties can be found when one party acts for the other even more zealously than the other might demonstrate, such as when a good friend dramatically defends you against a minor insult."[15] With high IBT, "a collective identity develops; we empathize strongly with

---

13. Lewicki and Tomlinson, "Trust, Trust Development, and Trust Repair," 113.
14. Lewicki and Tomlinson, "Trust, Trust Development, and Trust Repair," 108.
15. Lewicki and Tomlinson, "Trust, Trust Development, and Trust Repair," 109.

the other and incorporate parts of their psyche into our own identity (needs, preferences, thoughts, and behavior patterns)."[16]

High IBT and collective identity are heard in familiar sentiments:

- "You never leave a man behind."
- "Semper Fidelis."
- "Blood is thicker than water."
- "Always stick up for your friends, even when you know they're wrong."

In everyday terms, if I have high IBT toward you, I am likely to *have your back* and defend your actions. "This mutual understanding is developed to a point that each person can effectively act for the other."[17]

Related to this, the higher the IBT between us—i.e., the higher our *positive emotional attachment*—the more likely I am to rationalize and excuse your behavior. In everyday terms, when you do something immoral or unethical, I am more likely to:

- *turn a blind eye.*
- *look the other way.*
- *cover for you.*

EXTREME IBD: HATE CAN BE MORE THAN JUST HATE

To restate the earlier definition, IBD is "a confident negative expectation regarding another's conduct. It is grounded in perceived incompatibility of values, dissimilar goals, and negative emotional attachment to the other."[18] IBD can be low or high.

Breaking this definition down and magnifying it, my high IBD toward you is grounded in:

16. Lewicki and Tomlinson, "Trust, Trust Development, and Trust Repair," 109.
17. Lewicki and Tomlinson, "Trust, Trust Development, and Trust Repair," 109.
18. Lewicki and Tomlinson, "Trust, Trust Development, and Trust Repair," 112.

- *Perceived incompatibility of values*—My beliefs, religious views, morals, skin color, political affiliation—i.e., the ingredients that make up my identity—are incompatible with yours. I believe your values and beliefs are a threat to mine.

- *Perceived dissimilar goals*—On many levels, perhaps around desired outcomes, relationships, and processes, we are dissimilar. Your difference you want to make in the world is at least dissimilar, and quite possibly in conflict, with mine.

- *Negative emotions*—My negative perceptions of you are more emotion based than reason based. I may fear you and dislike you more than I rationally disagree with you.

- *Attachment*—This may be the most impactful term in this definition. If you and I are attached, we are interdependent. We are not merely coexisting. Your existence impacts me, and we are incompatible on an identity level.

The concept of identification-based distrust suggests how hate, at least at extremely high levels, can be more than just hate. It combines identity-level incompatibility with negative emotions and, perhaps most significantly, interdependent attachment. We can't help but affect each other. Your very existence represents a threat to me.

Collective Distrust: Hate Groups

One group can build a strong collective identity, and a strong mutual trust in one another, founded on that group's shared identification-based distrust toward another group.

Stated differently, I and others like me can form a powerful, like-minded community founded upon our shared distrust of you and yours. Further, this community is knit together and motivated by our negative emotional assessment of you all, and our perception that you place our shared identity at risk.

We hear this collective identity based on collective distrust in the following terms, and the groups that proclaim them:

- Western chauvinism
- You will not replace us
- Jews will not replace us
- White nationalism
- Ethnic cleansing

As individual terms, high IBT, collective identity, and high IBD are obscure and tedious. Together they help explain the disturbing differences some want to make in the world.

WHEN IBT IS VIOLATED: BETRAYAL

Trust violations occur when another person's behavior does not conform to expectations.[19] High trust may become low trust, or jump from trust to distrust. Violations of CBT, such as when a dry cleaner over-starches a shirt, have different consequences than violations of IBT, such as when a one friend *backstabs* another, or a spouse has an affair. Violations of CBT may be viewed as merely annoying, depending on the relationship. Though potentially serious, violations of CBT are "not likely to affect our emotional well-being over the long term."[20]

Violations of IBT, however, affect a person's identity. Hence, violations of IBT are more difficult to address and repair than violations of CBT. "The parties are likely to feel upset, angry, violated, or even foolish, if loss of face is a result of trusting the other when trusting turned out to be inappropriate."[21] In addition to these effects on personal and social identity, Lewicki includes how violations of IBT may disrupt or even end the shared identity of the parties on both sides of the violation.[22] "When the parties either fail to reconcile the trust violation with their shared identity or

---

19. Lewicki, "Trust, Trust Development, and Trust Repair," 107.
20. Lewicki, "Trust, Trust Development, and Trust Repair," 107.
21. Lewicki, "Trust, Trust Development, and Trust Repair," 108.
22. Lewicki, "Trust, Trust Development, and Trust Repair," 108.

are unable to do so, high-IBT relationships may be transformed to low IBT or even IBD."[23]

FORGIVENESS AS AN ACT OF POWER

> *The weak can never forgive. Forgiveness is the attribute of the strong.*
>
> —Mahatma Gandhi

Violations of IBT, depending on their severity, can be painful and disruptive on many levels. Given this, overcoming such a violation and moving forward, Lewicki and Tomlinson note, often involves some form of forgiveness.[24] But forgiving—be it another person, or oneself, or a group such as a team or company—is far from an obvious, straightforward process. "We advance and retreat, make progress and falter."[25] No two processes of forgiveness are alike, and the study of trust certainly does not reveal any standard ritual for how to proceed.

But forgiving someone is an act of individual power, or "bringing about desired outcomes," when the person forgiving is ready. The study of power clarifies some of the challenges faced, reveals aspects of authentic forgiveness, and presents a few subtle options for those who are considering forgiving another.

Forgiveness Is My Own Act of Individual Power

Forgiveness is not an act of social power, but rather "a process undertaken by one person in relation to another, with or without interaction with that person."[26] I forgive at my own discretion, in my own time, under my own power. Forgiving someone at their urging, or the urging of someone else, may well be inauthentic and violating in itself. Forgiveness scholar and pastoral counselor Gary

---

23. Lewicki and Tomlinson, "Trust, Trust Development, and Trust Repair," 125.
24. Lewicki and Tomlinson, "Trust, Trust Development, and Trust Repair," 124.
25. Hawk, email interview response, March 9, 2020.
26. Hawk, "Practice of Forgiveness and Reconciliation," 324.

W. Hawk sternly cautions against forcing forgiveness: "Requiring forgiveness or prescribing it in a therapeutic session may be at best untimely and at worst cause additional harm to the injured party."[27]

Any inclination to leverage forgiveness is particularly concerning in power-imbalanced settings, and settings involving high or involuntary dependence, such as teacher-child or parent-child. "A child's need for physical and emotional support may make children particularly prone to forgive and reconcile, especially when the person with greater power uses coercion."[28] Making the child forgive, or telling them they have a responsibility to forgive, "more often than not, creates another layer of harm that the child may carry into adulthood."[29]

To say that forgiveness is an act of individual and not social power requires clarification from a second angle. Forgiveness is not a means to intentionally change the behavior of another, but rather "an inside job with no requirements from another human being."[30] If one person says to another "I forgive you for what you did to me" with the intention of influencing them, this is likely a veiled attempt to manipulate.

Forgiveness Does Not Require Reconciliation

"Forgiveness neither obligates one to reconciliation nor necessitates it."[31] Where forgiveness is an act of individual power, apart from relationship, reconciliation is a careful act of social power that must take place within the relationship.

> Reconciliation is a process of re-establishing relationship, renewing trust, and settling differences so that cooperation and a sense of harmony are restored. Reconciliation brings parties together in a way that forgiveness cannot. For this reason, in speaking of forgiveness and reconciliation, it is

27. Hawk, "Practice of Forgiveness and Reconciliation," 325.
28. Hawk, "Practice of Forgiveness and Reconciliation," 324.
29. Hawk, "Practice of Forgiveness and Reconciliation," 324.
30. Hooks, *Power of Forgiveness*, ix.
31. Hawk, "Practice of Forgiveness and Reconciliation," 324.

essential to emphasize that forgiveness does not necessarily re-establish a relationship.[32]

Forgiveness and Adjusting Dependence

Forgiveness confronts involuntary dependence; it is an act of freeing oneself from the one who caused the harm. Consider an example from the movie *The Princess Bride*. The character Inigo Montoya is describing a memory of a six-fingered man who killed his father and wounded Inigo when he attempted to avenge his father's death:

> [I was] almost eleven, and when I was strong enough I dedicated my life to the study of fencing so that the next time we meet I will not fail. I'll just go up to the six-fingered man and say, "Hello, my name is Inigo Montoya, you killed my father, prepare to die."
>
> —Inigo Montoya

While Inigo's mission may appear noble, it must be set against the fact that the six-fingered man now controls his life, and has since age eleven. Inigo's whole identity—his ambitions, character, and sense of worth—has been consumed with the need for revenge. He has long been involuntarily dependent on the six-fingered man.

The benefits of forgiveness over revenge begin to crystallize when examined through the lens of dependence. Forgiveness offers a path to greater or complete independence, where revenge sweetly demands that dependence be prolonged and intensified. Indeed, revenge entices me to do and be the same as the person who violated me. This is precisely the appeal of revenge. Inigo Montoya has dedicated his life to being very much like the man he seeks to kill, only more so.

Forgiveness is a step toward healing an identity-level wound, where revenge seeks to create another that complements the first. Just pondering forgiveness brings with it the opportunity to think about what dependence on that person has looked like, should look like in light of violated IBT, and can look like moving forward.

32. Hawk, "Practice of Forgiveness and Reconciliation," 324.

Forgiveness and Adjusting Trust

Forgiveness does not require resuming the same level of trust, in the same way it does not require returning to the same level of dependence. The relationship does not, should not, and simply cannot return to what it was before. You need never speak to me or rely on me again. As noted, trust violations that involve forgiveness are those based on IBT specifically. This form of trust, "grounded in perceived compatibility of values, common goals, and positive emotional attachment to each other,"[33] is not set in stone. Neither forgiveness nor reconciliation require that a relationship return to what existed before. The person forgiving may choose a calculus-based, *arm's-length* relationship only, or none at all.

Forgiveness and Identity

Perhaps most profoundly, because IBT and identity are so closely interwoven, forgiveness may well involve reassessing aspects of one's own identity. Who am I now? Am I a different person as a result of this violation? How will forgiveness change who I am? Does forgiveness change my ambitions, needs, what I want to be known for, my values, or my concerns? Will forgiveness solidify or validate or reignite something within me? A victim of sexual assault, for example, may find new purpose in volunteering for a victim support service. A father who has thought about shaking his own baby may be the best person to talk to other men expecting their first child.

This implies a frank identity- and forgiveness-related question. Has *not* forgiving affected my identity, perhaps in ways I don't like? Am I the person I want to be? Has the harm done to me pulled me from my dreams and ambitions? How are my values and character being affected?

Assessing the effects on one's own identity may be the most daunting aspect of forgiveness. Indeed, forgiveness may be so hard precisely because it involves pondering how I am not the same person I was before the violation, and before the voluntary act of

---

33. Lewicki and Tomlinson, "Trust, Trust Development, and Trust Repair," 112.

forgiveness. This process, and the power inherent in it, is summarized well by Hawk:

> *Forgiveness is not a sign of weakness. Choosing to forgive another person may plunge one into the deepest reflection about who one is and how that identity is maintained. It requires us to consider who we are, independent of what has been done to us and independent of who the other person thinks we are. Forgiveness requires an act of imagination because it invites us to consider a future that is not merely a reaction to the past. Forgiveness requires us to undertake a long journey. It cannot possibly be for the faint of heart.*[34]

WHEN IBD IS VIOLATED: BEST PICTURE

Lewicki and Tomlinson stress that while trust can be violated, distrust can be as well. "We can expect trusting behavior and encounter distrust, or we can expect distrusting behavior and encounter trust."[35] CBD can transition to CBT, such as when a once-disappointed patron returns to a restaurant and is pleasantly surprised by the experience. A state trooper may pull me over not to give me a speeding ticket, but instead to let me know my right rear tire needs air.

The violation of IBD that results in IBT, however, resonates on a deeper level. Violating this form of distrust involves a transition from a *negative emotional attachment* and *perceived incompatibility of values* to a *positive emotional attachment* marked by *common values* and mutual identification. Can this actually happen? Is it realistic to expect one person to move from deep contempt for another person to a deep, trusting, respectful identification, even to a point where "a collective identity develops; we empathize strongly with the other and incorporate parts of their psyche in our own identity (needs, preferences, thoughts, and behavior patterns)"?[36]

    34. Hawk, "Practice of Forgiveness and Reconciliation," 323.
    35. Lewicki and Tomlinson, "Trust, Trust Development, and Trust Repair," 119.
    36. Lewicki and Tomlinson, "Trust, Trust Development, and Trust Repair," 109.

While such a thorough transformation may seem rare or even unrealistic, this is the plot of the movie *Toy Story*. This is, in fact, the story line of many movies, including a surprising percentage of Oscar Best Picture winners: e.g., *Crash*, *Chicago*, *West Side Story*, *Driving Ms. Daisy*, *Million Dollar Baby*. All hinge on just this tension and profound identity transformation from distrust to trust among the characters. There is much power in the violation of distrust.

11

Given Authority Versus All Other Types

> *We no longer live in a day in which the pastor is given authority just by virtue of the title. That change is probably good for us. Now we must earn the authority to speak into someone's life.*
> —Max Lucado, author of *Anxious for Nothing: Finding Calm in a Chaotic World*[1]

Authority—like power and trust and identity—is one word with many meanings. Max Lucado offers insights into two when contrasting *given* authority and *earned* authority. To help distinguish different types of authority, and the different types of power inherent within them, it helps to look at the word that comes immediately before or after—e.g., *given* authority, *an* authority, authority *figure*.

- Has someone been *given* authority, meaning another party has designated some form of exclusive, legitimate power to her?[2]
- Is he endorsed as *an* authority, meaning others recognize his established expertise?

1. Dyck, "Glad You Asked," 3.

2. This author treats given authority as synonymous with designated power and legitimate power.

Given Authority Versus All Other Types

- Do others endorse him as speaking *with* authority (Greek: *exousia*)? That is, do others agree that he communicates with legitimate certainty and established ability?
- Does she *exercise* authority (Greek: *exousiazo*) as a master would towards her slave, perhaps just to remind the slave she has this power?
- Does he *abuse* authority, meaning he somehow misuses designated legitimate power for his own gain?
- Does she act according to her *own* authority, such as when a company founder gives herself the title of president? Parents give themselves authority by becoming parents.
- Has she *earned* authority? Has she built up with them a blend of high IBT and high IBD, giving her the unique influence to, in Max Lucado's words, "speak into someone's life"? In other words, has she earned the right to address issues around identity: *Who am I? Who should I be? Should I be approaching my life differently?* (Note that earned authority is bestowed by others.)

Stephen Covey Sr., author of *The 7 Habits of Highly Effective People*, contributes two other forms of authority—*natural* authority and *moral* authority.[3] As he does, he continues this pattern of emphasizing the word adjacent to authority in order to distinguish it. He names natural authority as "the power given to humans to steward the rest of creation," and moral authority as describing the reciprocal relationship between a principled leader and principled followers.[4]

While an exhaustive understanding of authority requires a study of its own, the study of power aids in this understanding, and in the discernment between differing forms of authority. This is especially true related to *given* authority, the most common form of authority, and the most recognized form of power.

---

3. Covey, Foreword, Greenleaf, *Power of Servant Leadership*, 5.
4. Covey, Foreword, Greenleaf, *Power of Servant Leadership*, 5.

Section 2: Power in Context

GIVEN AUTHORITY AND COERCIVE POWER

All forms of authority are trust based, e.g., testifying as *an* authority, or speaking *with* authority. Given authority is similarly *entrusted* to a person.

But given authority is very often *reinforced* by formal distrust-based, i.e., coercive, power, "the legitimate right to threaten punishment for nonconformity."[5] A referee can call a foul, or eject a player. A city inspector can fine or even close a restaurant for violating health code. A parent can send his child to time-out. Consider how many forms of coercive power, including violent coercive power, a police officer might carry on her belt—gun, taser, mace, stick, handcuffs. She has been entrusted with all these sources of distrust-based power, and *authorized* to use any of them.

But the officer would likely much prefer to use her (trust-based) communications skills to bring about a peaceful resolution. Coercive power is ideally just the stick that makes the carrot more enticing. Though Al Capone was famous for operating outside the law, he was describing law enforcement well when he said, "You can get much farther with a kind word and a gun than you can with a kind word alone."

THE ETERNAL YESTERDAY: FIVE SOURCES OF GIVEN AUTHORITY

A pivotal question within given authority settings is, "Who gave you this authority?" Given authority can be designated from five directions:

- Given authority can come from those who will be *under* that authority, such as when a city elects a mayor and a nation elects its president and members of congress

- Given authority can come from those who will be *peers*, such as when a state medical board grants a license to practice, or police cadets are sworn into the force.

---

5. Raven and French, "Bases of Power," 154.

- Given authority can also be granted by those who will be *over* that authority, such as when a university president hires a head football coach.
- Strongly held authority can be given *from before*, by tradition or history. Max Weber refers to this source as "the 'eternal yesterday,' i.e. of the mores sanctified through the unimaginably ancient recognition and habitual orientation to conform. This is 'traditional' domination exercised by the patriarch and the patrimonial prince of yore."[6] Others have defined tradition as "peer pressure from dead people." Raven and French, while noting how this source of authority may be based on such characteristics as gender, caste, and physical characteristics, call attention to Weber's specific example of old age: "In some cultures, the aged are granted the right to prescribe behavior for others in practically all behavior areas."[7]
- Finally, ownership allows a person to designate authority to oneself, *from within*, such as when a company founder names herself president, or when a child appoints himself Very Stable Supreme Commander of the cardboard box spaceship he has created.

Setting-Based Power as Self-Endorsing

Chapter 3 presented ecological power, normative power, and designated power as forms of setting-based power, power best understood as a factor of the setting itself. Pondering how authority can be given from above and from peers and from tradition begins to reveal how these three can form a mutually sustaining set. Ecological power and normative power can combine to establish how power is designated and to whom. And in turn, designated power, in the highly visible form of given authority, can be the active agent by which to maintain existing normative power and ecological power. These three complement one another to maintain homeostasis in a

---

6. Roberts, "Extracts from Max Weber, " lines 519– 21.
7. French and Raven, "Bases of Power," 153.

Section 2: Power in Context

group: *It's tradition. That's the way we've always done it. Don't step out of line.* Power does depend on context, but context may well depend on setting-based power.

IS GIVEN AUTHORITY *MY* AUTHORITY?

Given authority may be the most recognized form of authority, and the most recognized of all forms of power. "The President of the United States, police, the chairperson of the PTA, the student government leader, your boss at work, all are designated power by their position."[8]

However, when examined through the lenses of endorsement, trust, and coercion, given authority is revealed to be foundationally distinct from other forms of authority. Further, it becomes distinct from other forms of power.

To clarify, several factors combine to make given authority look and feel like individual power, which belongs to the person, rather than social power, which is subject to ongoing endorsement within the relationship.

First, given authority is endorsed in advance, often formally. A mayor is ceremoniously sworn in when taking office, with cameras rolling. When a new regional director is hired to the position, a memo is sent out from those above her, celebrating her appointment and bestowing her authority. Hence it is understandable for a person with given authority to refer to it as a possession, as *my* authority.

All other forms of authority, and all other forms of social power, are endorsed within the interaction, in the moment. *Earned* authority, for example, is the ongoing symptom of a candid, vulnerable relationship. Someone regarded as *an* authority on a topic may not be recognized until someone introduces them as such, and even then their credentials may be disputed. If, for example, someone referred to themself by saying "I am an authority on this topic" or "I have earned authority with this group of people," others may consider this person arrogant or self-aggrandizing. But someone with given authority may say, "My authority gives me the

---

8. Hocker and Wilmot, *Interpersonal Conflict*, 9th ed., 107.

right to make this policy." Others may be required to accept that self-understanding.

(Returning to Covey's *natural* authority, anyone who has ever tried to teach a dog to fetch, or tried to keep a houseplant alive, appreciates that this form of authority is also subject to ongoing endorsement. The dog may just look at you. The houseplant may still die. The saying *You can lead a horse to water but you can't make it drink* reflects this natural truth.)

Given authority resembles individual power, appearing to belong to the one with that authority, for other key reasons:

- Given authority is often given by people removed, and not by those *under* that authority. A schoolteacher is given authority by his district, not his students. College students don't hire or fire their professors. Prison inmates don't elect their guards.

- Given authority is indisputable in the moment, within a specific setting. A basketball referee's whistle controls the game—a player who doesn't obey it gets ejected. But after the final buzzer, that whistle carries no authority. A federal court judge has near-total authority within her courtroom, but no more than anyone else at the grocery store.

- Those with given authority can use coercive power, sometimes even violence, at their discretion. A prison guard can use deadly force if he believes the situation warrants it in the moment. A first-grade teacher can take away a student's cell phone.

These factors combine to make given authority look and feel like individual power rather than social power. Even those people under a person's given authority may regard it as *her* authority, especially if they gave it to her, perhaps through election.

But a number of general cautions must accompany the perception that given authority belongs to that person:

- Given authority is still subject to ongoing endorsement. "Legitimate power stems from the willingness of others to accept an individual's direction."[9]

---

9. Vecchio, "Power, Politics, and Influence," 72.

- Given authority may simply not be understood. A foreign traveler may not know local curfew laws. A football player may not hear the whistle to stop play. "Regardless of how tight a hold a party may attempt to have on any resource, the resource is always used in the context of a relationship. It is the other party's view of the resource that makes it a basis for influence."[10]

- Is the given authority being obeyed, or is the coercive power behind it being endorsed? If a burglary suspect does not resist when arrested, is he obeying the authority of the arresting officers, or reacting to their coercive power?

- Given authority can be taken away. Elections remove or endorse given authority. A baseball coach can be fired. A school principal might not have her contract renewed.

- Given authority can be deliberately ignored or skirted. A racing driver may *bend the rules* involving car weight and horsepower. A local construction company may seek to *grease the palms* of local building inspectors.

DON'T EXPECT TOO MUCH FROM GIVEN AUTHORITY

For the teacher, given authority is needed for classroom control. For the coach, it helps when enforcing team rules. A driving instructor must have the authority to fail a student.

But these coercive steps contradict all other forms of power necessary in these expansive settings. Expertise, referent power, communication skills—these trust-based forms of power facilitate the expansive purposes of a teacher, coach, or parent. To resort to coercion and punishment as a primary, first-option source of power is to reduce an expansive setting like a classroom to being merely about control.

---

10. Folger, et al., *Working Through Conflict,* 146.

Given Authority Versus All Other Types

Endorsement of given authority is obedience only, not internalization. Given authority is power to demand compliance to a binary, yes/no standard. Stop when the light is red. Be marked tardy if you're not in your seat when the bell rings. A speed limit sign delineates numerically between obedience and disobedience. Given authority can enforce:

- classroom attendance but not classroom accomplishment,
- compliance to a code but not honoring a code,
- the rules of the game but not the spirit of the game,
- minimum responsibility but not maximum effort.

Those who have been given authority can pass laws related to gun control, such as making the gun buyer responsible for obtaining the standard background check instead of the seller. But ending gun violence is an outcome that the clumsy, binary power of given authority simply cannot achieve.

Racism won't end by making specific racist acts against the law. An unwanted pregnancy is the direct result of a lack of restraint by a male during intercourse, not due to the legality or illegality of abortion.

Many desired outcomes simply cannot be achieved through given authority and the coercive power to punish. It requires a consumeristic regard to expect gun violence and racism to be resolved by elected officials and law enforcement.

How Is Given Authority Taken Away?

Key to appreciating how given authority settings differ is assessing the processes by which given authority is *withdrawn* in each.

- When authority has been designated *from above*, such as when a manager is hired by the company owner, removing that authority may be as simple as saying "you're fired."
- When authority has been designated by *peers*, such as when a mandatory state bar association approves a lawyer to practice

in that state, removing that authority is often a longer, hidden, formal process. The review and removal process of a tenured professor may take a year or more, and that professor may be allowed to continue in her role during this process.

- When authority is given by those who will be *under* that authority, such as when electing a governor or president, removing that authority will require election or impeachment.
- When authority is granted by tradition/history, taking that authority away may require centuries, or revolution.
- Removing authority granted to someone by his *own* authority may be impossible. The only way to withdraw endorsement is to leave that setting.

TWO IRONIES OF GIVEN AUTHORITY

Irony 1: Legitimate power is given away as a means of gaining power.

When authority is given, this is a deliberate process of giving legitimate power away in order to increase the power of the group doing the giving. When a newly elected mayor takes the oath of office, it involves some form of promise to serve those elected. When a university hires a new football coach, it is to produce a better team for the university. A municipal judge is appointed to assess the enforcement of the law for the good of that municipality. As Hannah Arendt said, "Power is never the property of an individual; it belongs to a group and remains in existence only so long as the group keeps together."[11] Her words are never more valid than when they refer to given authority specifically.

Irony 2: Given authority exists to increase the power of the group *under* that authority.

The reason authority is given, regardless of whether it is given from above, or by peers, etc., is to increase the power of those assembled under that authority. This irony is true of any instance of given authority: prison guard, coach, county sheriff, schoolteacher,

---

11. Arendt, *On Violence*, 44.

GIVEN AUTHORITY VERSUS ALL OTHER TYPES

or army general. A county sheriff, for example, is given authority to keep the peace, i.e., to help residents of that county to live peacefully. The college football coach may inspire individual players, but if the team fails to win, he should expect to have his authority removed.

Prison guards may illustrate this irony best. Guard duties may include strict control of inmates, including catching and punishing individual rule-breakers. But all this is done foundationally to provide a safe, controlled setting for the inmate group as a whole to serve out their time. Prison guards exist foundationally to benefit of those who abide by the prison's rules. Controlling those who break the rules is merely a means to this end.

If I equate my given authority merely with control and the right to give orders, and punish and perhaps use deadly force, then I foundationally and dangerously misunderstand my authority, why it was given, and whom it is meant to benefit. Further, I am more likely to abuse that authority.

On the other side, if I am *under* someone's given authority, and I assume that person's role exists merely to control and coerce me, and as a result I instinctively distrust them, I fail to appreciate how that person's role exists for my sake. If I, for example, categorically distrust or even hate police officers, I egregiously misunderstand the extent of their role in my community.

Any instinctive resistance to given authority is especially limiting, and ironic, in expansive settings. If I instinctively dislike or distrust my teachers, how much do I limit myself and my opportunity? If a high school basketball player ignores the coach's direction, the whole team suffers. The teacher's given authority exists only to manage the setting precisely so that students can take advantage of it.

AUTHORITY: BRIDGING TRUST AND DISTRUST

Returning to Lewicki and Tomlinson's scholarship on trust dynamics (see chapter 10), they describe how trust and distrust often coexist, and sometimes in high levels, within the same relationship. This coexistence may be difficult to envision:

> Thus, just as trust implies the belief in the other, a tendency to attribute virtuous intentions to the other and willingness to act on the basis of another's conduct, distrust implies fear of the other, a tendency to attribute sinister intentions to the other, and a desire to protect oneself from the effects of the other's conduct.[12]

Further, Lewicki and Tomlinson describe how both trust and distrust exist in different forms: calculus-based trust and distrust (CBT and CBD) and identification-based trust and distrust (IBT and IBD). In short, if the coexistence of trust and distrust in the same relationship were not difficult enough to grasp, add to it that both trust and distrust manifest in different forms.

Given Authority: Balancing CBT and CBD

The interwoven tension between trust and distrust may be difficult to comprehend. But straightforward examples of these complex dynamics present themselves plainly in the study of authority. Specifically, those with given authority live in the tension between calculus-based trust and calculus-based distrust. The state trooper is aware that highway commuter may at once trust and distrust her to do her job. High school students may at once trust and distrust the given authority of their principal. In both these instances, the coexisting trust and distrust are not personal. The principal and the state trooper are just doing their jobs, and those responding to their authority are benefiting.

Earned Authority: Balancing IBT and IBD

Where the person with given authority balances calculus-based trust and calculus-based distrust to perform their role, someone with earned authority must aggressively steward the tension between identification-based trust and identification-based distrust. Returning to Max Lucado's distinction:

---

12. Lewicki and Tomlinson, "Trust, Trust Development, and Trust Repair," 111.

Given Authority Versus All Other Types

> We no longer live in a day in which the pastor is given authority just by virtue of the title. That change is probably good for us. Now we must earn the authority to speak into someone's life.[13]

For a person to earn authority to "speak into someone's life," that person must first develop a high level of identification-based trust. For you to foster earned authority, I must identify with you, and trust that you identify with me. We have *compatible values* and share a *positive emotional attachment*.

But your earned authority also places my identity at risk. You may challenge me to be a different person, give up certain self-destructive behaviors, change some aspect of my character, or question some aspect of my reputation. In short, my identity is not safe with you.

Many familiar terms exist that name this process of identity change—transformation, growth, learning, coaching, correction, stretching, maturing. And any of these can be unpleasant as they are happening. If my actions are unethical or immoral, and you confront me, I may feel some level of *negative emotional attachment*, precisely because our values and goals are incompatible in that moment. In this way, for you to earn authority to speak into my life, you must carefully and diligently earn both my identification-based trust and my identification-based distrust.

13. Dyck, "Glad You Asked," 3.

12

Self-Imposed Dangers of High Power

Straying from an intent focus upon others can catapult you toward selfish and shortsighted behavior, and the kind of abuses of power that fill the pages of daily newspapers, history books, biographies, and the work of Shakespeare and many other great authors.

It isn't just the wealthy and famous who can be undone by the seductions of power; it's any one of us at any moment. To lose focus on others can lead to empathy deficits and loss of compassion, impulsive and unethical action, and rude and uncivil behavior.

This is the heart of the power paradox: the seductions of power induce us to lose the very skills that enabled us to gain power in the first place.

—Dacher Keltner,
The Power Paradox: How We Gain and Lose Influence

Self-Imposed Dangers of High Power

THE POWER PARADOX: KELTNER

Power is "the ability to bring about desired outcomes."[1] Power is "the ability to change the behavior of others."[2] "The overwhelming evidence seems to indicate that the powerful tend to like power, use it, justify having it, and attempt to keep it."[3] "Power is a dopamine high."[4]

All these factors make it reasonable to believe the more power the better. Those with competitive and comparative regards may well find much satisfaction in high power status compared to others. But high power comes with numerous cautions.

As Lord Acton argues, power tends to corrupt, and absolute power tends to corrupt absolutely. Keltner's pointed conclusions above, drawn from decades of research, support Acton's argument. And earlier scholars also provide studied agreement. David Kipnis, social psychologist and author of *The Powerholders*, drew on his and others' research to assemble four *metamorphic effects of power* which describe how "successful influence changes the powerholder's views of others and of himself."[5] David McClelland, author of *Human Motivation*, describes how some people with high power "have a tendency to dominate others in an attempt to satisfy one's own hedonistic desires."[6] As Abraham Lincoln said, "Nearly all men can stand adversity, but if you want to test a man's character, give him power."

Why? Why might *keeping up with the Joneses*, or even passing them, cause me to lose compassion for them? Why does a sense of power, even in the moment, beckon me toward rude and unethical behavior, testing my identity? Why does a term like schadenfreude—the pleasure taken in another person's misfortune—even exist?

One tentative answer to these questions is that human nature exists within the context of nature, and nature is a competitive arena.

1. Coleman, "Power and Conflict," 1st ed., 112.
2. Vecchio, *Leadership*, 69.
3. Coleman, "Power and Conflict," 124.
4. Keltner, *Power Paradox*, 7.
5. Kipnis, *Powerholders*, 168.
6. Deutsch and Coleman, *Handbook of Conflict Resolution*, 117.

SECTION 2: POWER IN CONTEXT

METAMORPHIC EFFECTS OF POWER: KIPNIS

Kipnis lamented how "successful influence changes the powerholder's views of others and of himself, regardless of whether the actors involved are, say, a husband who continually dominates his wife or a great political leader who is responsible for the well-being of a nation."[7] Kipnis presented four unconscious "metamorphic effects of power":

1) *An overriding, zero-sum taste for power.* "This Hobbesian view suggests that the individual is driven by a fear that others may achieve equality with him in power and so deprive the individual of his power."[8] "The urge to be 'number one' becomes the exclusive preoccupation of the powerholder. When faced with a choice between giving up power and maintaining it by less than moral or legal methods, those with a taste for power choose the second option."[9]

2) *Corrupt abuse of legitimate power.* "When this form of corruption is under examination, one usually finds the powerholder in a position of trust, where he has access to institutional resources or the resources of another person. What seems to happen is that access to these resources tempts the powerholder to line his own pocket."[10]

3) *Perceived freedom from norms and morality.* Here Kipnis draws on the conclusions of Sorokin and Lundin, who found that "persons holding great power develop an exalted and vain view of their own worth which inhibits compassion for others."[11] Furthermore, "powerful persons evolve new codes of ethics that serve to justify their use of power. Throughout history, we find that a special divinity is assumed to surround the powerful, so that they are excused from gross acts of murder, terrorism and intimidation."[12] Donald Trump described this metamorphic effect in 2005, when he bragged to friends, "You know, I'm automatically attracted to beautiful—I just start kissing them. It's like a magnet. Just kiss. I don't even wait. And when you're a star, they let you do it. You can do anything."

- 7. Kipnis, *Powerholders*, 170.
- 8. Kipnis, *Powerholders*, 171.
- 9. Kipnis, *Powerholders*, 171.
- 10. Kipnis, *Powerholders*, 172, citing Sorokin and Lundin, *Power and Morality*.
- 11. Kipnis, *Powerholders*, 172.
- 12. Kipnis, *Powerholders*, 172.

"The very possession of vast power tends to demoralize [i.e., remove moral sense from] the powerholder."[13] Hence, the powerholder is free from the constraints of "commonly held norms and values," including ethical and basic civil behavior.

Kipnis notes that biased endorsement from those around the powerholder, perhaps in the forms of flattery, adulation, and eager agreement with the powerholder's opinions, may aid this untethered self-perception.

4) *Degradation and objectification of those less powerful.* "A fourth meaning assigned to the idea that power corrupts refers to the belief that powerholders devalue the worth of the less powerful and act to increase social distance from them."[14] "The less powerful become objects of manipulation with a lesser claim to human rights than is claimed by the powerholder."[15] Kipnis voices a shared concern among fellow psychologists: "the possibility that the very act of successfully influencing causes devaluation of the target person."[16]

TWO KINDS OF HIGH-POWER PEOPLE: MCCLELLAND

McClelland labels an individual's need for power as *nPower*, describing a person with a high need for power as *high nPower*. Such a person will "experience great satisfaction in influencing other people and arousing strong emotions in them."[17] "Individuals high on *nPower* seek out positions of authority."[18]

McClelland also presents two contrasting reasons why this power is desired. A person with high *nPower* and a *socialized power orientation* may seek to use her power "for the good of a cause, an organization, or an institution."[19]

13. Kipnis, *Powerholders*, 176.
14. Kipnis, *Powerholders*, 176.
15. Kipnis, *Powerholders*, 176.
16. Kipnis, *Powerholders*, 176.
17. Coleman and Deutsch, *Handbook of Conflict Resolution*, 117.
18. Coleman and Deutsch, *Handbook of Conflict Resolution*, 117.
19. Coleman and Deutsch, *Handbook of Conflict Resolution*, 117.

SECTION 2: POWER IN CONTEXT

In contrast, someone with *high nPower* and a *personalized power orientation* is "exemplified by a tendency to dominate others in an attempt to satisfy one's hedonistic desires."[20]

FUTURE ABUSE: BEFORE I KICKED THE DOG

Keltner and Kipnis describe ways high power can corrupt, or more specifically how the *successful use of power* can result in some form of corruption. McClelland concludes that I may seek high power due to preexisting "hedonistic" motivations.

Another possible source of corruption merits consideration: What happened a short time ago? What happened at the office to agitate me enough to kick the dog when I get home? Why does my wife *take it out on the kids* after an argument with her sister?

Conclusions across four very widely differing studies point to how a person's negative experiences in one setting lead them toward hostile, even abusive behavior in a near-future setting:

- Kids who feel neglected by dad are more likely to bully their peers.[21]

- After upset losses by the home professional football team, domestic violence incidents increase noticeably.[22]

- Young or single parenthood, stress, unstable family situations, depression, and history of mistreatment as a child—each of these factors increase the likelihood that parents or caregivers will forcefully shake a baby.[23]

- Those who self-report as "high-anger drivers" experience more trait anger, anxiety, and impulsiveness, and often describe being angry before driving.[24] "Perhaps from work or home stress,

---

20. Coleman and Deutsch, *Handbook of Conflict Resolution*, 117.
21. Christie-Mizell et al., "Bullying Behavior," abstract.
22. Card and Dahl, "Family Violence and Football," abstract.
23. "Shaken Baby Syndrome," lines 41–50.
24. "Fast and the Furious," lines 18–30.

high-anger drivers are more likely to get in the car angry; they also tend to express their anger outward and act impulsively."[25]

In each of these varied settings, a party experiencing some form of harm in one setting takes their anger out in a near-future setting. Further, the four examples above of this *future abuse* dynamic suggest that the abusive party is a low-power party in the initial setting and the high-power party in the subsequent setting.

THE DANGERS OF LOW POWER

> *The poor man looks upon the law as an enemy, not as a friend.*
>
> —Robert Kennedy

High power tends to corrupt, but low power tends to corrupt as well. "Too much losing does not build character; it builds aggression, or apathy. Most examples of retaliation occur because the person doing the retaliating perceives himself or herself to be in a low-power position."[26] "Powerlessness amplifies the individual's sensitivity to threat; it hyperactivates the stress response and the hormone cortisol; and it damages the brain. These effects compromise our ability to reason, to reflect, to engage in the world, and to feel good and hopeful about the future."[27]

"When you are low power in a relationship that matters, you may feel a sense of low self-esteem, of feeling worthless or unable to influence your situation. You may feel sad, defeated, or depressed."[28] In fact, Keltner's studied concerns lead him to conclude:

> *Powerlessness, I believe, is the greatest threat outside of climate change facing society today.*[29]

---

25. "Fast and the Furious," lines 29–30.
26. Hocker and Wilmot, *Interpersonal Conflict*, 138.
27. Keltner, *Power Paradox*, 7.
28. Hocker and Wilmot, *Interpersonal Conflict*, 126.
29. Keltner, *Power Paradox*, 10.

SECTION 2: POWER IN CONTEXT

SCHUTZ'S FIRO-B: YOUR POWER MEETS MY NEEDS

McClelland's conclusions state that some people want high power, either to achieve their own selfish identity goals or for the good of the group. But others don't want high power so much as they want other people to employ power on their behalf.

Schutz's FIRO-B (Fundamental Interpersonal Relations Orientation-Behavior) instrument differentiates these preferences on a group level. The FIRO-B assesses my needs from the group in three areas: need for inclusion, need for affection, and need for control.[30] It breaks each of these needs down into two complimentary assessments: (a) my desire to meet these needs and (b) my desire to have others meet these need on my behalf. Hence the FIRO-B assesses these behaviors on a total of six spectrums:

Need for Inclusion:

1. My desire to include others
2. My desire to be included by others

Need for Control:

3. My desire to control others
4. My desire to be controlled by others

Need for Affection:

5. My desire to show affection for others
6. My desire to have others show affection to me

All six FIRO-B assessments describe power bids. Each examines how I want power to work within the group, so that my needs are met. You may gain esteem primarily by making others feel

---

30. Griffin, "FIRO Theory of Needs," 93–96.

included, while I gain esteem primarily from experiencing others wanting to include me. In this way, all six assessments describe relational outcomes I desire. For example, this assessment may reveal that you:

- score high on *expresses inclusion*,
- score low on *wants inclusion*.

These two scores (of the six) reveal you aren't concerned about others including you, and you like including others. In contrast, my FIRO–B score may reveal that I:

- score high on *wants inclusion*,
- score high on *expresses control*.

These two of my six scores reveal I want others to invite and include me without me asking, and I want to run the group once I'm in it.

CONSUMERISM: SOCIETY'S POWER ON MY BEHALF

Schutz's FIRO–B theory describes group-level relationships. He describes in collaborative terms how some members of a group want high power, and some, for all intents and purposes, prefer low power.

> *It may be hard for the movers and shakers of this world to understand, but Schutz's FIRO theory recognizes that some people have a desire to be submissive and dependent, to have their paths laid out by others. Viewed negatively, these people with an inclination to empower others can be seen as wimps. A more charitable judgment is that they are trusting, respectful, obedient, and willing to serve.*[31]

Schutz cautions to not just assume some people are wimps because they want to be submissive and dependent, and it would be more charitable to regard them as trusting, respectful, and obedient.

31. Griffin, "FIRO Theory of Needs," 94.

Section 2: Power in Context

Peter Block, surveying power on a societal level, brings a decidedly less charitable regard to those who prefer *to have their paths laid out by others*. Block sums this up in his contrast between *citizens* and *consumers*:

> [Regarding citizens] Our definition here is that a citizen is one who is willing to be accountable for and committed to the well-being of the whole. That whole can be a city block, a community, a nation, the earth. A citizen is one who produces the future, someone who does not wait, beg, or dream for the future.
>
> The antithesis of being a citizen is the choice to be a consumer or a client . . . Consumers give power away. They believe that their own needs can be best satisfied by the actions of others—whether those are elected officials, top management, social service providers, or the shopping mall. Consumers allow others to define their needs. If leaders and service providers are guilty of labeling or projecting onto others the "needs" to justify their own style of leadership or service they provide, consumers collude with them by accepting others definition of their needs. This provider-consumer transaction is the breeding ground for entitlement, and it is unfriendly to our definition of citizen and the power inherent in that definition.[32]

Consumers bring about their desired outcomes by finding those who do want power, either for their own sake or for the good of those around them, and placing expectations and obligations upon them. A consumer hears the admonishment "With great power comes great responsibility" and responds, "Yes, exactly."

DESTRUCTIVE SYMBIOSIS

Chapter 2 described ecological power, normative power, and designated power as forms of *setting-based* power. These forms of power control and define the domains in which individuals negotiate other forms of power.

---

32. Block, *Community*, 63.

Self-Imposed Dangers of High Power

However, if settings can influence the behavior of the individuals within them, individuals can impact the settings they are within as well. Revolutions, elections, and regime changes are familiar mechanisms by which individuals seek to *deliberately influence* setting-based power: to change the context. Individuals and groups can also effectively harm or even destroy the setting, or make it uninhabitable. Pollution, overgrazing, and climate change are familiar examples of individual power damaging the setting it exists within.

Reconsider Block's description of how leaders and consumers collaborate:

> *If leaders . . . are guilty of labeling or projecting onto others the "needs" to justify their own style of leadership . . . consumers collude with them by accepting others' definition of their needs.*[33]

This collaboration between consumers and leaders, if concerned solely with the individual needs and wants of each, gravitates toward a state of *minimal* or even *destructive symbiosis*. Demonstrating a state of destructive symbiosis, consumers and their leaders may collaborate around getting their individual needs and wants met, which may well include those the setting—be it an ocean, a local ecosystem, or a planet—cannot sustain.

Two Cautions When Diagnosing Consumerism

Two cautions must accompany any discussion of consumerism:

1. Those with low power aren't necessarily consumers. Most people who sense low power want more power, in order to live the life they want. One way to determine whether those with low power actually want low power is to attempt to empower them. Then observe their response. Consumers don't want to be empowered.
2. Those with high power—e.g., money, status, stature—may well prefer to be consumers. Indeed, money helps achieve

33. Block, *Community*, 63.

consumer status. Consumers are willing to pay money, perhaps a great deal of money, to bestow obligations on others and achieve consumer status.

WITH GREAT POWER MUST COME GREAT RESTRAINT

> *What lies in our power to do, lies in our power not to do.*
> —Aristotle

In October of 2019, American troops were ordered to pull out of the region surrounding Qamishli, Syria, where they had for years allied with Syrian Kurds to fight ISIS. As a convoy of around one hundred armored vehicles, most with large gun turrets mounted on top, drove slowly through crowded Qamishli streets, betrayed Kurds pelted them with potatoes and rotten vegetables.

The troops in the vehicles, though the power at their fingertips could obliterate the civilians, instead endured the embarrassing attack without responding. And they were right. Had they responded with the power available to them, had they *returned fire*, even briefly, they and their country would have been guilty of a heinous crime against humanity.

"With great power comes great responsibility," goes the saying popularly attributed to Spider-Man's Uncle Ben, but also heard in similar forms for centuries. Implicit within this: with great power must come great restraint. The greater my power is compared to yours, especially my violent power, the more I must resist resorting to it. Might does not make right, nor does it give me the right. A toddler hitting his mother as hard as he can does not justify the mother returning the blow. The one with greater power must demonstrate that power precisely by not striking back.

SELF-IMPOSED DANGERS OF HIGH POWER

THE IRONY OF *HENRY V*

> *Kings have no friends, just subjects and enemies.*
> —George R. R. Martin

Those with high power, and high legitimate power specifically, may find themselves effectively powerless when it comes to certain deeply desired outcomes, such as simple friendship and camaraderie. This is because power imbalance creates face threat; i.e., those with low power are often uncomfortable and guarded around those with high power. Hence the very goals a high-power party values most—friendship, candor, honesty—may be unachievable due to that high power itself.

The reality television series *Undercover Boss* relies on this dynamic as its hook. In this series, company owners and top executives don disguises—literally hiding their faces—and become entry-level employees. They then engage fellow employees from a low-power position. In this way, high legitimate power parties receive unvarnished insights into their company policies, processes, and performance. But they gain poignant awareness of their employees' circumstances as well, including strengths, hopes, challenges, and struggles. Further, these disguised leaders often learn difficult lessons about themselves—i.e., their true social identities—from their employees.

Such candid, vulnerable community is not possible without hiding their high legitimate power.

Call this *The Irony of Henry V*, after the king in Shakespeare's play. In act 4, scene 1 (a black predawn scene) King Henry borrows a cloak from an officer because the night is cold. His head covered and face hidden, he sits down at a fire among members of his infantry. There he engages in an argument with these "commoners." They freely question the king's identity, their loyalty to him, and his loyalty to them. Even the hidden Henry contributes; he describes a condition that would lead him to stop trusting the king.

So this hidden king experiences candid community among his subjects. The conversation culminates with King Henry being slapped across the face by one of his own subjects for presuming the king would care what Henry thinks.

By deceiving, King Henry gains complete, bracing honesty. Does he have this right, even with his own troops? Is he dishonoring them, or honoring them? Do Henry's good intentions justify the deception?

Regardless, by hiding his immense legitimate power, Shakespeare's good king gains something he keenly desires: heartfelt, robust, candid community. These were the very joys he had sought out in his youth, before war. Indeed, at the beginning of the play some questioned whether he would make a good ruler precisely because these were the ends he desired as a young king.

Power is, among other things, "the ability to bring about desired outcomes," and "the ability to change the behavior of others." But the irony of Henry V demonstrates that high power itself can make some deeply desired outcomes unattainable, and change others' behavior in precisely the opposite ways the person with high power wants. The higher the power, the more that power may need to be hidden to achieve delicate outcomes like easy but honest friendship.

Bibliography

Angelou, Maya, and Bill Moyers. "A Conversation with Maya Angelou." In *Conversations with Maya Angelou*, edited by Jeffrey M. Elliot. Jackson: University of Mississippi Press, 1989.
Arendt, Hannah, *On Violence*. Orlando: Harcourt, 1970.
Ashforth, Blake E., and Fred A. Mael. "The Power of Resistance: Sustaining Valued Identities," In *Power and Influence in Organizations*, edited Robert M. Kramer and Margaret A. Neale, 89–119. London: Sage, 1998.
Bass, Bernard. "Concepts of Leadership." In *Leadership: Understanding the Dynamics of Power and Influence in Organizations*, edited by Robert P. Vecchio, 3–22. 2nd ed. Notre Dame, IN: University of Notre Dame Press, 2008.
Blanchard, Kenneth, and Spenser Johnson. *The One Minute Manager*. New York: Berkley, 1998.
Block, Peter. *Community: The Structure of Belonging*. San Francisco: Berrett-Koehler, 2009.
Braun, Eduardo P. "It's the Culture, Stupid." *Huffington Post*, June 2013. http://www.huffingtonpost.com/eduardo-p-braun/its-the-culture-stupid_2_b_3487503.html.
Brooks, David, *The Road to Character*, New York: Random House, 2015.
Brown, Penelope, and Stephen Levinson, *Politeness: Some Universals in Language Usage*. Cambridge: Cambridge University Press, 1987.
———. Email interview with author, October 2013.
Brundin, Jenny. "Colorado Teens Say School Stress, Phones, Social Pressure Are behind Growing Mental Health Issues." Colorado Public Radio, October 24, 2019. https://www.cpr.org/2019/10/24/colorado-teens-say-school-stress-phones-social-pressure-are-behind-growing-mental-health-issues/.
Card, D., and GB Dahl, "Family Violence and Football: The Effect of Unexpected Emotional Cues on Violent Behavior." *Quarterly Journal of Economics* 126/1 (2011) 103–43. https://www.ncbi.nlm.nih.gov/pubmed/21853617.
Christie-Mizell, et al., "Bullying Behavior, Parents' Work Hours and Early Adolescents' Perceptions of Time Spent with Parents." *Youth & Society* 43/4 (November 2010) 1570–95. https://journals.sagepub.com/doi/abs/10.1177/0044118x10388261.

BIBLIOGRAPHY

Coleman, Peter. "Power and Conflict." In *The Handbook of Conflict Resolution: Theory and Practice*, edited by Morton Deutsch and Peter T. Coleman, 108–30. 1st ed. San Francisco: Jossey-Bass, 2000.

———. "Power and Conflict." In *The Handbook of Conflict Resolution: Theory and Practice*, edited by Morton Deutsch et al., 108–30. 2nd ed. San Francisco: Jossey-Bass, 2006.

———. "Power and Conflict." In *The Handbook of Conflict Resolution: Theory and Practice*, edited by Peter T. Coleman et al., 137–67. 3rd ed. San Francisco: Jossey-Bass, 2014.

Collins, Jim. "Level 5 Leadership: The Triumph of Humility and Fierce Resolve." In *Leadership: Understanding the Dynamics of Power and Influence in Organizations*, edited by Robert Vecchio, 394–406. 2nd ed. Notre Dame, IN: University of Notre Dame Press, 2008.

———. "Why Business Thinking Is Not the Answer." Text excerpts from *Good to Great and the Social Sectors* (author's note). November 2005. http://www.jimcollins.com/books/g2g-ss.html.

Covey, Stephen, Sr. Foreword. In *The Power of Servant Leadership*, by Robert Greenleaf. 25th anniversary ed.. New York: Paulist, 2002.

Crouch, Andy. *Playing God: Redeeming the Gift of Power*. Downers Grove, IL: InterVarsity, 2013.

Deutsch, Morton. *The Resolution of Conflict*. London: Yale University Press, 1973.

Dyck, Drew. "Glad You Asked: Max Lucado on the Power of Questions, Pastoral Authority, and Giving a Firm Word of Correction." *Leadership Journal*, Summer 2011, 3. http://www.christianitytoday.com/le/2011/summer/gladyouasked.html.

"The Fast and the Furious." American Psychological Association, February 2014. https://www.apa.org/action/resources/research-in-action/rage.

Fisher, Max. "This Map Shows Where the World's 30 Million Slaves Live. There are 60,000 in the U.S." *Washington Post*, October 17, 2013. Online: http://www.washingtonpost.com/blogs/worldviews/wp/2013/10/17/this-map-shows-where-the-worlds-30-million-slaves-live-there-are-60000-in-the-u-s/.

Fiske, Susan. "Controlling Other People: The Impact of Stereotyping." *American Psychologist*, June 1993. http://www.radford.edu/~jaspelme/_private/gradsoc_articles/stereotypes%20and%20prejudice/Power_and_stereotypes.pdf.

Folger, Joseph P., Marshal Scott Poole, and Randall K. Stutman. *Working Through Conflict*. 6th ed. New York: Pearson, 2009.

Forsyth, Donelson. *Group Dynamics*. 5th ed. Belmont, CA: Cengage, 2009.

French, John R. P., Jr., and Bertram Raven, "The Bases of Social Power." 1959. https://www.researchgate.net/publication/215915730_The_bases_of_social_power.

Fuller, Robert W. *All Rise: Somebodies, Nobodies, and the Politics of Dignity*. San Francisco: Berrett-Koehler, 2006.

BIBLIOGRAPHY

Greenleaf, Robert. *The Power of Servant Leadership.* San Francisco: Berrett-Koehler, 1998.

———. "The Servant as Leader." In *Leadership: Understanding the Dynamics of Power and Influence in Organizations,* edited by Robert P. Vecchio, 407–15. 2nd ed. Notre Dame, IN: University of Notre Dame Press, 2008.

Griffin, Em. "FIRO Theory of Needs of William Schutz." In *A First Look at Communication Theory.* New York: McGraw-Hill, n.d. http://www.afirstlook.com/docs/firo.pdf.

Hathaway, Ashantai. "Boy in Touching Obama Photo Looks Back on Viral Moment." *TheGrio,* February 22, 2017. https://thegrio.com/2017/02/22/obama-boy-photo-touching-president-hair/.

Hawk, Gary W. "The Practice of Forgiveness and Reconciliation" In *Interpersonal Conflict,* edited by Joyce Hocker, 317–60. 10th ed., New York: McGraw-Hill, 2018.

Heath, Anthony. *Rational Choice and Social Exchange: A Critique of Exchange Theory.* London: Cambridge University Press, 1976.

Heimans, Jeremy, and Henry Timms. *New Power: How Power Works in Our Hyperconnected World—and How to Make It Work for You.* New York: Doubleday, 2018.

Hocker, Joyce. Email interview with author, April, 2011.

Hocker, Joyce, and William Wilmot. *Interpersonal Conflict.* 10th ed. New York: McGraw-Hill, 2018.

———. *Interpersonal Conflict.* 9th ed. New York: McGraw-Hill, 2013.

———. *Interpersonal Conflict.* 3rd ed. Dubuque, IA: Wm C. Brown, 1993.

Hofstede Center. "Power Distance Dimensions." http://geert-hofstede.com/dimensions.html.

Hopper, Elizabeth. "Maslow's Hierarchy of Needs Explained." *Thoughtco,* February 24, 2020. https://www.thoughtco.com/maslows-hierarchy-of-needs-4582571.

Jan, Tracy, "Redlining Was Banned 50 Years Ago. It's Still Hurting Minorities Today." *Washington Post,* March 28, 2018. https://www.washingtonpost.com/news/wonk/wp/2018/03/28/redlining-was-banned-50-years-ago-its-still-hurting-minorities-today/.

Johnson, Richard R. "The Psychological Influence of the Police Uniform." 2nd section. *Police1,* August 11, 2017. http://www.police1.com/police-products/apparel/undergear/articles/99417-The-psychological-influence-of-the-police-uniform/.

Keltner, Dacher. *The Power Paradox.* New York: Penguin, 2016.

Kerr, Michael, and Murray Bowen, *Family Evaluation: The Role of the Family as an Emotional Unit that Governs Individual Behavior and Development.* New York: Norton, 1988.

King, Martin Luther, Jr. "On Power and Love." Online: http://www.terraquote.com/tag/power-and-love/.

Kipnis, David. *The Powerholders.* Chicago: University of Chicago Press, 1979.

Bibliography

Kruse, Kevin. "100 Best Quotes on Leadership." *Forbes.com*, October 16, 2012. http://www.forbes.com/sites/kevinkruse/2012/10/16/quotes-on-leadership/.

Levinger, Gordon. "The Development of Perceptions and Behavior in Newly Formed Social Power Relationships." In *Studies in Social Power*, edited by Dorwin Cartwright, 83–98. Ann Arbor: University of Michigan Press, 1959.

Lewicki, Roy J., "Trust, Trust Development, and Trust Repair." In *The Handbook of Conflict Resolution*, edited by Morton Deutsch and Peter T. Coleman, 104–36. 1st ed. San Francisco: Jossey-Bass, 2000.

Lewicki, Roy J., and Edward C. Tomlinson. "Trust, Trust Development, and Trust Repair." In *The Handbook of Conflict Resolution*, edited by Peter T. Coleman et al., 104–36. 3rd ed. San Francisco: Jossey-Bass, 2014.

Lewicki, Roy J., and Carolyn Wiethoff. "Trust, Trust Development, and Trust Repair." In *The Handbook of Conflict Resolution*, edited by Peter T. Coleman et al., 86–107. 2nd ed. San Francisco: Jossey-Bass, 2006.

MacWilliams, Matthew. "The One Weird Trait That Predicts Whether You're a Trump Supporter." *Politico*, January 2016. https://www.politico.com/magazine/story/2016/01/donald-trump-2016-authoritarian-213533.

McKinney, Michael. "The Art of Leadership." *Leading Blog*, September 23, 2011. http://www.leadershipnow.com/leadingblog/2011/09/the_art_of_leadership.html.

———. "Leadership Quotes." *Leading Blog*, n.d. http://www.leadershipnow.com/leadingblog/leadershipquotes.html.

McKnight, John, and Peter Block. *The Abundant Community: Awakening the Power of Families and Neighborhoods*. San Francisco: Berrett-Koehler, 2010.

Milgram, Stanley. *Obedience to Authority: An Experimental View*. New York: Harper & Row, 1974.

Milne, A. A. *The House at Pooh Corner*. New York: Dutton, 1942.

Pettigrew, Thomas F. "Social Psychological Perspectives on Trump Supporters." *Journal of Social and Political Psychology* 5/1 (2017). https://jspp.psychopen.eu/article/view/750/html.

Pierro, Antonio, et al. "Bases of Social Power, Leadership Styles, and Organizational Commitment." *International Journal of Psychology* 48 (October 2012) 1122–34. https://onlinelibrary.wiley.com/doi/abs/10.1080/00207594.2012.733398.

Ragelienė, Tija. "Links of Adolescents Identity Development and Relationship with Peers: A Systematic Literature Review." *Journal of the Canadian Academy of Child and Adolescent Psychiatry* 25/2 (Spring 2016) 97–105. https://www.ncbi.nlm.nih.gov/pmc/articles/PMC4879949/.

Roberts, Andrew. "Extracts from Max Weber: The Protestant Ethic and the Spirit of Capitalism." *Studymore.org.uk*. http://studymore.org.uk/xweb.htm.

Bibliography

Senge, Peter M. *The Fifth Discipline: The Art & Practice of the Learning Organization.* New York: Currency Doubleday, 1990.

"Shaken Baby Syndrome." Mayo Clinic. https://www.mayoclinic.org/diseases-conditions/shaken-baby-syndrome/symptoms-causes/syc-20366619.

Skowron, Elizabeth, and Myrna Friedlander. "The Differentiation of Self Inventory: Development and Initial Validation." *Journal of Counseling Psychology* 45/2 (1998) 235–46. http://www.cabrillo.edu/~creyes/classes/Differentiation.pdf.

Steinke, Peter L. *How Your Church Family Works: Understanding Congregations as Emotional Systems.* Herndon, VA: Alban Institute, 1999.

Tan, S. Y., and Y. Tatsumura. "Alexander Fleming (1881–1955): Discoverer of Penicillin." *Singapore Medical Journal* 56/7 (2015) 366.

Ting-Toomey, Stella, and Leeva C. Chung. *Understanding Intercultural Communication.* Los Angeles: Roxbury, 2005.

Ury, William, Jeanne M. Brett, and Stephen B. Goldberg. *Getting Disputes Resolved: Designing Systems to Cut the Costs of Conflict.* San Francisco: Jossey-Bass, 1988.

Vanderbos, Gary R. "Identity." *APA Dictionary of Psychology.* https://dictionary.apa.org/identity.

Vecchio, Robert. "Introduction and Overview." In *Leadership: Understanding the Dynamics of Power and Influence in Organizations*, edited by Robert P. Vecchio, 1–2. 2nd ed. Notre Dame, IN: University of Notre Dame Press, 2008.

———. "Power, Politics, and Influence." In *Leadership: Understanding the Dynamics of Power and Influence in Organizations*, edited by Robert P. Vecchio, 69–95. 2nd ed. Notre Dame, IN: University of Notre Dame Press, 2008.

Weber, Max. *On Charisma and Institution Building.* Edited by S. N. Eisenstadt. Chicago: University of Chicago Press, 1977.

Whooley, Owen. "Collective Identity." *The Blackwell Encyclopedia of Sociology*, edited by G. Ritzer. February 15, 2007. https://onlinelibrary.wiley.com/doi/abs/10.1002/9781405165518.wbeosc065.

Yonack, Lyn. "Sexual Assault Is About Power: How the #MeToo Campaign Is Restoring Power to Victims." *Psychology Today*, November 14, 2017. https://www.psychologytoday.com/us/blog/psychoanalysis-unplugged/201711/sexual-assault-is-about-power.

www.ingramcontent.com/pod-product-compliance
Lightning Source LLC
Chambersburg PA
CBHW071431160426
43195CB00013B/1867